Making
WONDERFUL
SCRAPBOOK PAGES

It's Easier Than You Think

Page Designers

We are grateful to the following people for creating the album pages which appear in this book. Some of these designers have scrapbooking retail stores (see page 144). We're proud to feature their wonderful album pages. In alphabetical order, they are:

- **Kristy Banks** for Pebbles in my Pocket
- **Jenna Beegle**, Woodstock, Georgia
- **Ameberly Beck**, Lewiston, Idaho
- **Jane Blakesley**, Salt Lake City, Utah
- **Terri Carter** for Paper Hearts
- **Nancy Church** for Pebbles in my Pocket
- **Sally Clarke**, Portland, Oregon
- **Susan Cobb** for Hot Off The Press, Inc.
- **Carol Dace**, Des Plaines, Illinois
- **LeNae Gerig** for Hot Off The Press, Inc.
- **Becky Goughnour** for Hot Off The Press, Inc.
- **Katie Hacker** for Hot Off The Press, Inc.
- **Debbie Hewitt**, Agoura, California
- **Heather Hummel**, Salt Lake City, Utah
- **Melodie Jones**, Yurba Linda, California
- **Debbie Peterson**, Kennewick, Washington
- **Ann Smith** for Memory Lane
- **Anne-Marie Spencer** for Hot Off The Press, Inc.
- **Stephanie Taylor**, Paris, France
- **Shauna Wright** for Paper Hearts

Production Credits

Project Editors
Kris Andrews
Tara Choate
Mary Margaret Hite
Graphic Designers
Jacie Pete
Carmalee Roncketti
Susan Shea
Production Manager
Tom Muir

Photographers
Reed Anderson
Larry Seith
Digital Imagers
Victoria Gleason
Larry Seith
Editors
Lynda Hill
Paulette Jarvey
Teresa Nelson

More Great Hot Off The Press People

Accounting
Becky Christenson
Laura Gustafson
Wendy Irvine
Phil Jenkins
Angelique Smith
Janet Voeller
Sandi Weeks
Computer Systems
Daryn Edwards
Mike Jarvey
Steven Plant
Sales & Marketing
Heather Adair
Ed Eggling
Gail Hallbacka
Caralee Hutchinson

Pete Rutley
John Spiva
Special Assistants
Brenda Brãbender
Marty Hite
Patti Smith
Warehouse
Calley George
Juston Gleason
Chris Goughnour
Nathan Harner
Chad Hepner
Steve Jones
Steve Ocampo
Marnie Sievers
Randy Thomas

published by:

HOT OFF THE PRESS INC.

©1999 by **HOT OFF THE PRESS** INC. All rights reserved. No part of this publication may be reproduced or utilized in any form or by any means, including photocopying, without permission in writing from the publisher. Printed in the United States of America.

The information in this book is presented in good faith; however, no warranty is given nor are results guaranteed. Hot Off The Press, Inc. disclaims any liability for untoward results.

The designs in this book are protected by copyright; however, you may make the designs for your personal use or to sell for pin money. This use has been surpassed when the designs are made by employees or sold through commercial outlets. Not for commercial reproduction.

Hot Off The Press wants to be kind to the environment. Whenever possible we follow the 3 R's—reduce, reuse and recycle. We use soy and UV inks that greatly reduce the release of volatile organic solvents.

For a color catalog of nearly 300 craft and memory books, send $2.00 to:

HOT OFF THE PRESS INC.
1250 N.W. Third, Dept. B
Canby, Oregon 97013
phone (503) 266-9102
fax (503) 266-8749
http://www.hotp.com

HOT OFF THE PRESS INC.

HOTP 2199

Making
WONDERFUL
SCRAPBOOK PAGES

It's Easier Than You Think

- **228 scrapbook pages**
- **14 techniques**
- **over 100 punch ideas**
- **plus guidelines, hints & tips**
- **from the creators of**
  Making Great
  Scrapbook Pages

Table of Contents

All About Scrapbooking

We all have memories to share and stories to tell. Creating memory albums, or scrapbooking, gives each of us a unique way to do both. Let's get those wonderful photos out of shoeboxes and into albums where they can be shared.

Scrapbooking is easy to do. All you do is cut and glue! While there are many special tools and products, all you need is paper, scissors, glue and, of course, your photos! It's important to use acid-free and lignin-free papers, plus acid-free glues and pens. You'll want to keep your pages in acid-free sheet protectors so they won't become contaminated and ruin all your fine work.

You'll also need straight edged and patterned-edged scissors, plastic templates to help cut and crop in perfect circles, ovals, stars and other common shapes. Then you'll want an album or three ring binder to display your finished pages. Aside from these basic supplies, you can add stickers, die cuts, punches, patterned rulers, stencils, rubber stamps—the list of "nice-to-haves" could go on forever!

To help get you started, we've covered all the basic information you'll need in this chapter. Here are steps to build a page, basic cropping and matting techniques and ideas on how to journal. Pages 12 and 13 suggest six "rules" for making wonderful scrapbook pages! To make it easier for you to reproduce the techniques, we've listed the products used and the company who makes them next to each album page.

Note: Throughout this book, we've used Paper Pizazz™ patterned papers. Paper Pizazz™ is available in book form and by the sheet, although not every pattern is sold individually. We've listed the papers by name with the book title italicized in parenthesis—**Paper Pizazz™:** snowflake (Christmas).

This chapter's background paper is Paper Pizazz™ purple tiles sold only by the sheet.

Good, Better & Wonderful

Good

Better

Wonderful

The "good" album pages shown here have uncropped photos, simply attached to a white album page with a bit of journaling. A good beginning, but there's room to grow!

The "better" pages show how simple cropping and matting photos greatly improves the look (cropping and matting are explained in more detail on pages 10 and 11). We believe an album full of only better pages can be somewhat boring.

But just look at the difference adding patterned papers can make! Surprisingly, making "wonderful" pages doesn't have to take a lot of time. As you can see, a patterned background paper can make a world of difference and make it quickly and easily.

You may choose to make every page "wonderful," or every second or fourth page. The goal of this book is to give you the tools to quickly and easily create wonderful scrapbook pages!

Good

Better

Wonderful

How To Build A Page

—7 steps to a wonderful page

1 Select your photos based on the theme or event for your album page. You might think of each scrapbook page as having a story to tell.

2 Select plain and patterned papers to complement your photos. You might find a themed patterned paper that will mirror the story of your photos. Then choose colors to coordinate with the patterned paper. Or, as shown at the bottom of page 8, you may simply want to choose patterned papers with colors found in your photos. Pages 14–17 offer ideas for choosing and mixing papers.

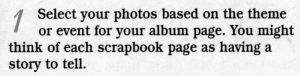

3 Crop your photos (more about this on page 10). Here a plastic template helps make a perfect circle.

4 Mat your photos with plain or patterned paper (page 11 goes into more detail about matting). Glue the cropped photos to the paper and cut ⅛"–½" away using plain or pattern-edged scissors.

5 Arrange the photos—pages 12 and 13 will offer some guidelines. Here we've mixed sizes and shapes for a pleasing arrangement.

6 Add decorative elements—Punch-Outs™, punches, stickers, die cuts, etc. These bugs and flowers are from *Paper Pizazz™ Charming & Cheerful Punch-Outs™*.

7 Last, journal. This is where you add words to finish your page's story. Keep it as brief or as involved as you think is necessary. You'll find more tips about this on pages 20 and 21. We've journaled on the mat. Now slip the completed page into a sheet protector, then into your album.

Cropping—think of it as clever cutting

You can freely crop your photos if you have the negative or a double print safely tucked away. Cropping photos allows you to get more photos per page and to make your pages more interesting.

1 Leave historical items like houses, cars or furniture—they'll be fun to see years from now.

2 Trim close to the focal person, place or thing. Use straight or pattern-edged scissors.

3 If you're hesitant about cropping older or one-of-a-kind photos, make a color copy (yes, a color copy is best even for black & white photos) and cut the copy for your album page.

4 Use a plastic template for smooth ovals, perfect circles and great shapes. Place the template on top of the photo and draw the shape on the photo with a pencil. Then cut inside the line. Lots of shapes are available.

5 **Silhouetting** is cutting around the person or object. This allows the focal point of the photo to stand out more on your album page. Cut along the edge of the focal point, removing all the background.

6 **Bumping out** one section of the photo is silhouetting one area, but leaving the rest of the photo with the background. This cropping technique works especially well with elbows, legs or balloons.

7 Yes, Polaroid photos can be cropped, just do not cut into the white envelope at the bottom of the photo. For freshly-developed photos, wait 10–15 minutes until they are completely dry before cropping.

Matting

1 Glue the cropped photo to a sheet of paper and cut ⅛"–½" away, forming a mat. Use plain or patterned paper for the mat. Use straight-edged scissors...

2 ...or pattern-edged scissors for one or both cuts. It's fun to mix and match cuts.

3 When matting a bumped-out cropped photo, it's good to keep the mat simple and cut close to the photo.

4 Double mat some photos, varying the sizes of the mats from narrow to wide.

5 Mix straight-edged and pattern-edged scissors on your photos and mats.

6 How about a triple mat, just for fun? Or quadruple mat, or more?

7 Mix your mat shapes, perhaps putting an oval inside a rectangle, a circle inside a square or a heart inside a diamond.

8 Journaling on a wide mat offers a great look!

A Few Basic Rules

#1 Establish a Focal Point

We often refer to the "focal point" of an album page—the one element which instantly attracts the eye. A page without a clear focal point lacks impact. Create a focal point by enlarging one of the photos, then place the focal photo in the center of the page with the other elements—photos or embellishments—around it.

Paper Pizazz™: diagonal appliqué on aqua (*Lovely & Lacy Papers*)
Solid Paper Pizazz™: metallic gold (*Metallic Papers*), white (*Plain Pastels*)
Punch-Outs™: "Our Wedding Day" (*Sayings*)
Decorative scissors: Victorian by Fiskars®, Inc.

#2 Vary the Photo Sizes

Mix photo sizes to add interest to your album pages. While the smaller page looks nice, the larger page is much more interesting. Enlarge one photo and vary the size of other elements, such as the journaling.

Paper Pizazz™: bright gathers (*Bright Great Backgrounds*), purple wiggle, blue large spirals (*Light Great Backgrounds*)
Bow and border punches: McGill, Inc.
Alphabet stickers: Frances Meyer, Inc.®

#3 Vary the Photo Shapes

An album page can be bland if the elements are too similar in shape. The left page is cute but all those rectangles make it hard to move from one photo to another. Changing the shapes of two photos helps carry the eye from one photo to the next.

Paper Pizazz™: pink & blue plaid (*Light Great Backgrounds*)
Solid Paper Pizazz™: yellow, pink, blue (*Plain Brights*)
Punch-Outs™: bunny, hearts, quilt (*Baby*)
Decorative scissors: leaf by Fiskars®, Inc.

#4 Overlap the Elements

Wonderful things happen when you overlap the elements! More photos or larger elements will fit on the page and your pages become more interesting. Overlapping the photos and other elements helps direct the viewer's eye and it provides plenty of space for the variety of shapes and sizes you've planned for your design.

Paper Pizazz™: white daisies (*Floral Papers*), burgundy handmade (*Pretty Papers*)

Solid Paper Pizazz™: dark green (*Solid Jewel Tones*), lavender (*Plain Pastels*)

Flower stickers: ©Mrs. Grossman's Paper Co.

Decorative scissors: colonial, arabian, Victorian by Fiskars®, Inc.

#5 Fill the Center

The center of the page attracts the eye first. If the center is blank, the page looks "blah." You can imagine this page without that center star—it would be okay, but lacking something. The journaled star helps link the photos and directs the eye toward the other elements.

Paper Pizazz™: pastel stripes, baby items (*Baby*)

Solid Paper Pizazz™: light blue, yellow (*Plain Pastels*)

Punch-Outs™: bunnies, bear, lamb, rattle, pacifier (*Baby*)

Decorative scissors: deckle by Fiskars®, Inc.

#6 *The Golden Rule*

There is a Golden Rule to using patterned papers: **mat your photos with plain papers.** *A plain mat provides a solid outline around your photos that visually separates them from the background patterned paper and makes them pop off the page. The sample page uses two patterned papers but even they are separated with a plain paper mat.*

Paper Pizazz™: tri-dots on pink, yellow and blue plaid (*Light Great Backgrounds*)

Solid Paper Pizazz™: yellow, blue (*Plain Pastels*)

Punch-Outs™: lamb, heart, bootie (*Baby*)

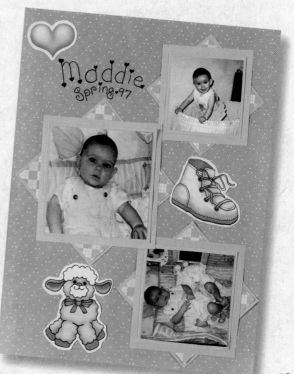

Using Patterned Papers

There are lots of ways to use patterned papers and many effects each can have, depending on how you use them. You only need to be a little daring. Just remember that Paper Pizazz™ papers have been designed to work together, and we'll help you with the daring part!

Choosing just the right patterned paper for your album page design may seem hard at first. We offer these guidelines as a way to help you begin. As you become more comfortable in creating your scrapbook, choosing patterned papers will become second nature!

Choose patterned papers to match the theme of your photos. The Autumn Leaves paper was chosen to carry the theme of the fall season shown in this family's photo. The solid paper colors used to make punched leaves and paper strips were pulled from the Autumn Leaves background paper.

Paper Pizazz™: autumn leaves (*Holidays and Seasons*)
Solid Paper Pizazz™: burgundy, dark green, brown, light brown (*Solid Jewel Tones*), yellow, orange (*Solid Muted Colors*)
Leaf punches: Family Treasures
Alphabet stickers: ©Mrs. Grossman's Paper Company
Metallic gold pen: Gel roller by Marvy® Uchida
Decorative scissors: deckle by Family Treasures

© & ™ Accu/Cut® Systems

Choose patterned papers to match the colors in your photos. Choose the brown swirl paper to pick up the brown, tan and black tones in the photos. Pull the solid paper colors used for matting and embellishing from the background paper. As you can see, all of the papers use the same tones as those found in the photographs. As long as the tones are the same, mixing the colors works! The gold pen lines, dots and swirls do a nice job of helping the colors blend.

Paper Pizazz™: brown swirl (*Black & White Photos*)
Solid Paper Pizazz™: dark brown, light brown, black (*Solid Jewel Tones*)
Suitcase die cut: Accu/Cut® Systems
Photo corners: Fiskars®, Inc.
Metallic gold pen: Gel roller by Marvy® Uchida
Decorative scissors: Pompeii Canyon Cutters by McGill, Inc.
Photographs: Front Street Photo

Often, new scrapbookers may feel intimidated using patterned papers on their pages. They might timidly use a bit of patterned paper as a photo mat with a solid paper for the background. The pages below demonstrate what a difference patterned papers make as backgrounds. Although both pages use the same elements, when the patterned papers are the background instead of a mat, the page has more Pizazz!

This page shows good use of choosing a patterned paper to match the colors of the photos. The striped paper matches the Christmas theme and the girls' clothes. But on this page, notice how the white mats blend with the white stripes in the second mat and how the red stripes blend with the red background. These photos are cute but more can be done!

Paper Pizazz™: red & white stripes, white dot on red (*Ho Ho Ho!!!*)
Solid Paper Pizazz™: white (*Plain Pastels*), red (*Plain Brights*)
Punch-Outs™: penguin, candy (*Christmas*)
Decorative scissors: wave by Family Treasures

Wow! Now these photos really pop! Those smiles are jumping out at you. The dot paper "reads" dark, which is why it works so well between the white mat and the striped background paper. The striped background paper really makes the page come alive. The journaling circle tells the story and the Punch-Outs™ offer a finishing touch. What a wonderful page!

Paper Pizazz™: red & white stripes, white dot on red (*Ho Ho Ho!!!*)
Solid Paper Pizazz™: white (*Plain Pastels*), red (*Plain Brights*)
Punch-Outs™: penguin, candy (*Christmas*)
Decorative scissors: wave by Family Treasures

Mixing Patterned Papers

Mixing patterned papers can be a lot of fun once you know how! After you understand the basic guidelines, there's really no trick to it. It's all about using light and dark color; the eye reads light and dark well together. The rest, if you follow The Golden Rule, takes care of itself.

Cutting a large shape, here an oval and rectangle, from each patterned paper gives you the center shape and the outer frame for each page. We call this the "2-for-1" technique. Simply glue the center shape into the frame of the second pattern.

These two patterned papers work well together because of the contrast between light and dark. Party hats was chosen to match the birthday theme. Lines & dots paper shares the primary colors of the party hats paper. The mat papers are chosen to match the colors of both patterned papers. They also help to visually separate the photos from the background.

Paper Pizazz™: party hats, lines & dots (*Birthday*)
Solid Paper Pizazz™: green, yellow, red (*Plain Brights*), navy blue (*Solid Jewel Tones*)
1" wide balloon punch: Family Treasures
½" wide balloon punch: Marvy® Uchida
Birthday die cut: Accu/Cut® Systems
Alphabet stickers: Frances Meyer, Inc.®
White pen: Gel roller by Marvy® Uchida
Decorative scissors: ripply by McGill

This page illustrates a great way to use non-themed patterned papers to design a birthday spread. The black plain paper becomes the second "patterned" paper with the addition of punched spirals and drawn white dots. The mat colors echo the primary colors of the focal photo and dot paper.

Paper Pizazz™: dots on purple (Child's Play)
Solid Paper Pizazz™: yellow, blue, red, green (*Plain Brights*), purple, black (*Solid Jewel Tones*)
Spiral punch: Frances Meyer, Inc.®
Alphabet and swirl stickers: Provo Craft®

Mix patterned papers by staying within the same color scheme. In this example, the plaid paper sets the color grouping. The other papers pick up the colors in the plaid. The plain dark green paper is a perfect contrast for the pastel grouping.

Paper Pizazz™: peach and mint plaid, tri-dots on peach, mint swirl (*Light Great Backgrounds*)

Solid Paper Pizazz™: dark green (*Solid Jewel Tones*), yellow, white (*Plain Pastels*)

Decorative scissors: deckle, sunflower by Fiskars®, Inc.

Reversible tulip punch: Marvy® Uchida

Mix patterned papers by using the same color combination. Each patterned paper uses hunter green and off-white. The pieced punched hearts include a bit of each patterned paper and look how well they work! The eye views each pattern separately, yet the colors link them.

Paper Pizazz™: green pinstripe, green with stars, green checks (*Dots, Stripes, Plaids & Checks*)

Solid Paper Pizazz™: dark blue, dark green (*Solid Jewel Tones*), white (*Plain Pastels*)

Heart and teardrop punches: Family Treasures

Alphabet stickers: Making Memories™

Small bow punch: Marvy® Uchida

Decorative scissors: deckle by Family Treasures

Blue and green pens: Zig® Writer by EK Success Ltd.

These patterns are easily mixed because they echo the pattern found in the baby's dress. The dress shows pink roses blooming on green vines. The pink roses patterned paper backed by the ivy paper just makes the baby pop off the page even more. Notice the roses are cut around the blooms to make this unusual mat. Any time you can recognize a pattern in the photos, you can be assured that it will work well in the background, too!

Paper Pizazz™: pink rosebuds, ivy (*Floral Papers*)

Solid Paper Pizazz™: pink (*Plain Brights*), burgundy (*Solid Muted Colors*)

Alphabet stickers: Frances Meyer, Inc.®

Silver pen: Zig® Opaque Writer by EK Success Ltd.

Photo Tips—

Take your camera with you everywhere and be always prepared with extra film and batteries. Remember, better photos equal better albums!

Hold the camera vertically to avoid cutting your subject off at the waist.

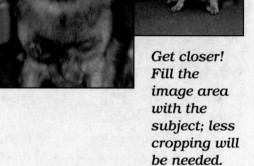

Get closer! Fill the image area with the subject; less cropping will be needed.

Include action in your photos. Take a sequence of photos or use high-speed film to capture the actions as it happens.

Take a second look at what you see in the view-finder. You'd be amazed at the things that sometimes "grow" out of a subject!

Ham it up! When taking "set-up" or posed shots, have people do more than just smile at the camera. A good picture is interesting even if you don't know the people in it.

Take photos of everyday activities. Don't wait only for holidays and birthdays. Capture your child in everyday life— bathing, playing, eating and sleeping.

Take lots of shots, not just one! Some will turn out better than others. Take the same scene from different distances: far away, closer, up close and personal!

Some common questions

These are a few questions scrapbookers often ask us. Through research of other scrapbookers and our own experiences, we've come to the following conclusions.

Q. Scrapbooking takes too much time. I have too many pictures and not enough time. How do I do it?

A. The best way to begin your scrapbook is to start with your most recent photos and work backwards. Every page does not have to be a time consuming masterpiece. Remember the primary reason for your scrapbook is to preserve your photos in a fun and attractive manner. To save time you might try pairing a more elaborate page with a very simple companion page. We believe using patterned papers makes the craft easier.

Q. Can I mix photos and color copies on a page?

A. Color copies may look a little different than the photos on your page, but they will blend in just fine. If you have only one print of a special photo, use a color copy for your album. The other advantage to using color copies is that you can easily manipulate the sizes needed for your page. Always color copy on acid-free paper.

Q. What size album page is better to use or create?

A. There is no right size, but we think it's best to use a standard size album, 8½"x11" or 12"x12". Scrapbookers use both size papers in either size albums. If you use a large 3-ring binder, both 8½"x11" and 12"x12" album pages can be placed into it.

Q. I used a magnetic album years ago and now my photos are stuck. How can I remove them?

A. Stretch dental floss under the photo and saw back and forth to remove the photos. Another idea is to heat the back of the page with a hair dryer to loosen the adhesive. Or carefully use a metal spatula to separate the photo and page.

Q. What causes "red eye" and how do I get rid of it?

A. Red eye is caused from the flash being too close to the camera lens. The red is the result of the light reflecting off blood vessels in the eye. To correct this, turn on the room lights so the pupils are contracted. When it does occur, use a red eye pen which removes it. A pet eye pen does the same thing, taking care of the unsightly green that comes from light reflecting off your pet's cornea.

Journaling Tips

While one picture may be worth a thousand words, there are some things that a photo just can't say. That's why journaling is such an important part of your album page design. It can finish the story that your photos tell.

Many people worry about how much to write. Some don't want to write much. They either hate their handwriting (we offer solutions for this in chapter 6), or don't know what to say. Others worry that they write too much. They fear the journaling won't be read if it's too long.

This is the easiest way to journal! Just write a sentence around each photo. The journaling is short and to the point, the writing small and fun. There's no need for perfection. The journaling also helps guide the eye to each photo. Give the information in the third person so even years from now, the viewers will know who and what the page features.

Paper Pizazz™: bright interlock, tie dye (*Bright Great Backgrounds*)
Solid Paper Pizazz™: orange, green, blue, yellow (*Plain Brights*) white (*Plain Pastels*), black (*Solid Jewel Tones*)
Bike, star, flower and spiral stickers: Provo Craft®
Decorative scissors: deckle by Family Treasures
White pen: Zig® Opaque Writer by EK Success Ltd.

The journaling here is a bit longer, but it's broken up into blocks to keep it easily accessible. Each bit of the story is placed close to the photo it explains. Writing as a "reporter" in the third person "he/Darian" or "she/Ari" form makes the story easier to read and fun for everyone. For years to come, viewers will always know that it was Uncle Darian and Niece Ari that had this fight...and that they made up!

Paper Pizazz™: ouch (*Childhood Memories*)
Solid Paper Pizazz™: yellow, red (*Plain Brights*)
Punch-Outs™: bandaids (*Kids*)

Page idea from the contest winner at the 1998 Great American Scrapbook Show in Dallas, Texas. We're sorry we don't have the winner's name!

Voice—who's writing vs. who's speaking

Often, scrapbookers wonder in what voice they should offer facts such as names, dates or stories. Since journaling provides the historical perspective of your photos, it's easier to answer this question!

"Third person" voice traditionally works best. In both examples below the voice is in third person form. It helps both stories remain relevant when read by someone other than who is in the photos. Even if you're making an album for your child, use the third person voice and call him or her by name. "Billy loved riding bikes" will be meaningful whether he reads it in 10 years or his grandchildren read it in 40 years. "You loved riding your bike" will eventually become unclear.

When journaling longer stories, even if you plan to mat it in small blocks, you may want to use a typewriter or computer. It helps the page look neater, and it's probably easier to read.

This page is designed to look like a newspaper page. The journaling is in a single column with captions below some photos, much like you would see in a newspaper. A "third person" tells the story, referring to the people by name like a reporter would do. This journaling will serve the family well, no matter how many years go by. The viewer will always know this page shows the adventurous great-grandma Jean, whereas great-grandchildren may not know who the "I" in "I had always dreamed of wanting a motorcycle" is.

Paper Pizazz™: blue wiggle (*Great Backgrounds*)
Solid Paper Pizazz™: white (*Plain Pastels*)

Here, the journaling is more elaborate. While it could have been kept in one block, the poem is broken up and matted in separate stanzas below the appropriate photo. The last two lines of the poem indicate the page is a gift from one sister to another; therefore, the designer didn't think it necessary to actually name each girl. Yet she still used the third person voice so that anyone who read it could enjoy the story.

Paper Pizazz™: watercolor pansies (*Watercolor Papers*)
Solid Paper Pizazz™: blue, burgundy, green (*Solid Jewel Tones*)
Butterfly punch: Family Treasures
Decorative scissors: clouds by Fiskars®, Inc.

What a Great Mix!

It's not a secret that patterned papers can make a good album page great! Of course, we feel the best looks can be had with Paper Pizazz™ patterned papers. We know that mixing patterned papers is an art that, while it may come naturally to some, is a learned art for most of us. This chapter is presented in a question and answer format with an album page example to demonstrate each answer. We hope it will prove invaluable to you when you begin to explore mixing patterned papers and designing your album pages with Pizazz!

If you're wondering if there's a limit to the number of patterned papers you can use in one design, the example at the bottom of page 27 will offer one answer. If you're not sure how to combine color schemes of patterned papers, the examples at the bottom of page 26 and the top of page 29 will help! And if you're not sure where to begin with choosing papers, the example at the top of page 26 and the bottom of page 28 will offer suggestions.

Aside from answering your most frequently asked questions, this chapter also shows you some basic techniques for matting, embellishing with pens, using Punch-Outs™ and adding die cuts or stickers. You'll see that patterns don't have to be cut only from solid papers (page 28), and that elements from a patterned paper can be cut and used as a decorative addition to your page (page 29). A basic technique for designing a two-page spread is shown at the bottom of page 27, and silhouette cutting is shown at the top of page 27.

So, in this chapter you'll find answers to commonly asked patterned paper questions and some wonderful album pages. What a great mix!

This chapter's background paper is from Paper Pizazz™ Light Great Backgrounds.

© Disney Enterprises, Inc.

How can you mix these two patterned papers?

The outdoorsy flannel has little to do with the trains moving across the rugged landscape, and certainly nothing to do with the photos; however, the bright red of the flannel matches the train. Matting the photos on solid black provides separation. Finally, adding train stickers to the outer circle ties the papers together.

Paper Pizazz™: red & black plaid (*Masculine Papers*), trains (*Disney's Magic Kingdoms*)
Solid Paper Pizazz™: black (*Solid Jewel Tones*)
Letter & train stickers: Frances Meyer, Inc.®
Decorative scissors: zipper by Fiskars®, Inc.
Page designer: LeNae Gerig for Hot Off The Press

© Disney Enterprises, Inc.

Shouldn't you use only the colors from the background paper?

Sometimes a page will look better with another color added. The seashells paper provides the perfect background for these photos, but it doesn't bring out the photo colors. The square spirals paper has lots of blue to accent the ocean, as well as orange to link it to the seashells paper.

Paper Pizazz™: seashells (*Embossed Papers*), square spirals (*Bright Great Backgrounds*)
Solid Paper Pizazz™: black (*Solid Jewel Tones*), brown, orange (*Solid Muted Colors*)
Starfish die cuts: Accu/Cut® Systems
Page Designer: Katie Hacker for Hot Off The Press

© & ™ Accu/Cut® Systems

If you use a bright, busy background paper, do you need to use duller papers around the photos?

Bright papers won't overwhelm your photos, so you don't need to worry about using them as mats. The cars & planes paper, with the colorful stripes paper matting it, provides lots of choices for mats. This combination works because the colors match and only ½" of the stripes paper shows around the edges, allowing the cars & planes paper to be the focus. The matting papers link the firecracker, rocket and colorful dots paper to the background.

Paper Pizazz™: colorful stripes (*Birthday*), cars & planes (*Child's Play*), colorful dots (*School Days*)
Solid Paper Pizazz™: red, blue, yellow (*Plain Brights*)
Punch-Outs™: rocket, fire truck (*Kids*)
⅜" wide circle punch: Fiskars®, Inc.
Decorative scissors: peaks by Fiskars®, Inc.
Page Designer: Amberly Beck

Should you limit yourself to one or two patterned papers on a page?

By using patchwork techniques, unrelated papers (perhaps they were even paper scraps) work together. On this page, borders surround each patterned piece and the use of punches embellishes the theme. (Bunny punch pattern on page 34.)

Paper Pizazz™: yellow & blue stripes, mint with dots, tri-dots on pink, light blue lines & dots, blue argyle (*Dots, Checks, Plaids & Stripes*)
Solid Paper Pizazz™: white, yellow, mint (*Plain Pastels*)
⅞" wide heart, bow, border and corner punches: McGill, Inc.
½" wide egg, tulip, butterfly and duck punches: Marvy® Uchida
Decorative scissors: deckle, sunflower by Fiskars®, Inc.
Pink pens: Zig® Writer by EK Success Ltd.
Page designer: Debbie Peterson

How can you use four patterned papers together?

Three of these papers share a pink-and-blue color scheme, but their pastel shades allow them to work on the mint paper too. Combine the papers into patchwork balloons, then use spiral punches to tie the other elements together one last time!

Paper Pizazz™: mint tri-dots, tri-dots on pink, light blue lines & dots, pastel stripes on pink (*Dots, Checks, Plaids & Stripes*)
Solid Paper Pizazz™: white, yellow (*Plain Pastels*), gray (*Solid Muted Colors*)
Balloon stencil: Westrim® Crafts
Spiral punch: Family Treasures
Decorative scissors: deckle, colonial by Fiskars®, Inc.
Blue and pink pens: Zig® Writer by EK Success Ltd.
Page designer: Debbie Peterson

Must the patterned papers have something to do with the photos?

Not necessarily! The red & black plaid paper, which looks a lot like flannel, is great for the outdoor photos. The gold spirals bring out the yellow in the photos while the same paper repeats the black in the plaid paper. Cut the trees (which reinforce the theme in the photos) from the center of the paper first, then use the outer paper for a page mat.

Paper Pizazz™: spirals on black (*Bright Great Backgrounds*), red & black plaid (*Masculine Papers*)
Solid Paper Pizazz™: red, black (*Solid Jewel Tones*)
Tree templates: Provo Craft®
Gold pen: Gel Roller by Marvy® Uchida
Page designer: LeNae Gerig for Hot Off The Press

How do you choose papers in a color scheme and know they will mix?

Select papers with similar colors in each of them. Here, black and gold are found in all three papers, with two of them (the metallic dots and strips) also having copper and silver.

Paper Pizazz™: metallic dots, metallic stripes, metallic gold (*Metallic Papers*), gold borders (*Black & White Photos*)
Decorative scissors: deckle by Family Treasures
Page designer: Katie Hacker for Hot Off The Press

Can papers with large patterns be used only as background sheets?

Background papers are intended to be used as one large sheet, so when you cut out a piece of the pattern the result can be really unique! The swirling music staff has been cut from its background and placed on black paper matted on gold. The crushed suede paper picks up the copper color and provides a subtle background.

Paper Pizazz™: crushed suede (*Black & White Photos*), metallic music notes, metallic stripes (*Metallic Papers*)
Solid Paper Pizazz™: metallic gold, metallic copper (*Metallic Papers*), black (*Solid Jewel Tones*)
Decorative scissors: heart-strings by Fiskars®, Inc.
Gold pen: Zig® Writer by EK Success Ltd.
Page designer: Anne-Marie Spencer for Hot Off The Press

Laurence and Anne-Marie

Punches
Wanna Make Something of It?

Scrapbookers are constantly looking for new and unique ways to use paper punches. We've pooled the creative resources of our designers to come up with the following chapter packed full of wonderful theme-related shapes you can create. Each of them requires punches to make, but often only the most basic shapes. So, if you don't already have circles, hearts, stars and balloon punches, they'll be easy to find at your scrapbooking retailer!

This chapter contains over 130 designs you can make with common punch shapes. Each idea is diagramed so you can see exactly which punch shapes are combined to create the new idea! You'll see precisely where to cut, glue, overlap, or draw. All diagrams are proportional—this means you can make the design with any size punch as long as they are in proportion to each other.

Also, simply because we created a tiny clown face out of tiny hole punches, doesn't mean that you must be limited by that! You can make clowns as large as the largest punch you can find. Scale the designs to fit your needs. Since we use common punches, you can easily substitute a large square shape in the place of our small one!

Some of the punch characters you will find in this chapter are put to use on pages throughout the book. While we have included a few album pages in this chapter to illustrate our use of these punch creations, many can be found in other chapters of this book. Just keep your eyes peeled for them as you read along. If you find a great punch design in another section of the book it will be referenced in this chapter so you'll be sure to find the diagram to recreate it for use on you own wonderful scrapbook page!

This chapter's background paper is from *Paper Pizazz*™ *Bright Great Backgrounds*.

"My Buds" page by Heather Hummel.

29

Basic Instructions

 = Cut  = Draw 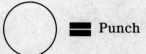 = Punch ————— = Overlap

For Example: Peppermint by Jenna Beegle

 +  + 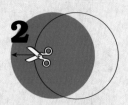 =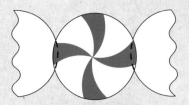

You will need a plain white circle...

and... another white circle, cut in half with a wiggly line or with pattern-edged scissors...

and... two red circles, each punched as shown. Then cut each crescent in half.

Glue the pieces together as shown.

Circle Punches

Apple by Jenna Beegle

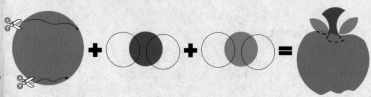

Bubble Gum by Susan Cobb

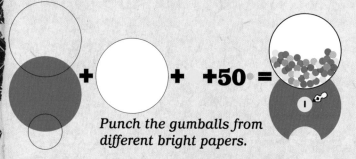

Punch the gumballs from different bright papers.

Watermelon by Jenna Beegle

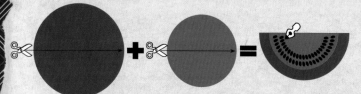

Cherries by Jenna Beegle

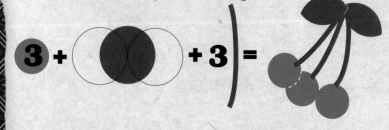

Candy Corn by Debbie Hewitt

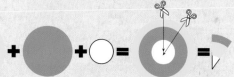

Tomato by Susan Cobb

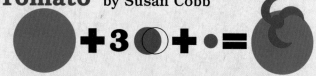

Grapes by Jenna Beegle

Pizza by Debbie Hewitt

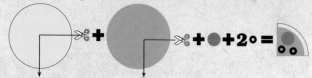

Orange by Jenna Beegle

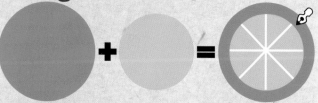

Lemon by Jenna Beegle

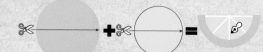

Sundae by Susan Cobb

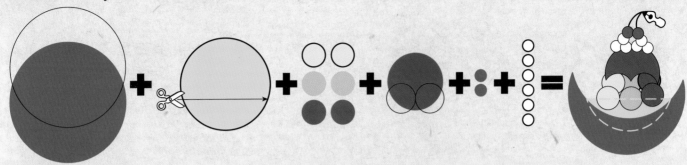

Sunflower by Debbie Hewitt

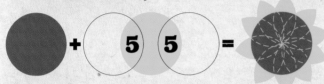

Daffodil by Jenna Beegle

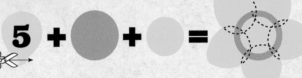

Flower by Debbie Hewitt

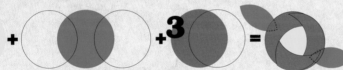

Daisy by Jenna Beegle

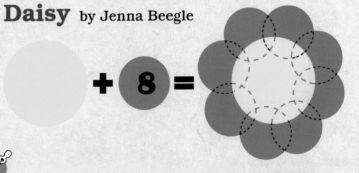

Turtle by Susan Cobb

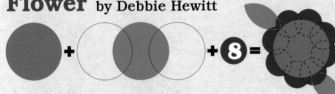

Bat by Susan Cobb

Camellia by Debbie Hewitt

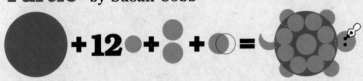

Flamingo by Susan Cobb

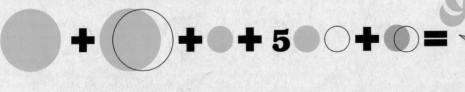

Clown by Jenna Beegle

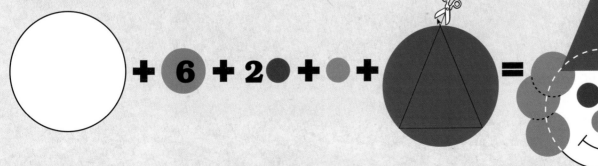

Baby by Jenna Beegle

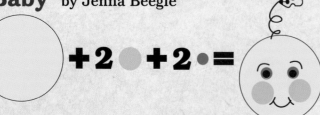

Face by Jenna Beegle

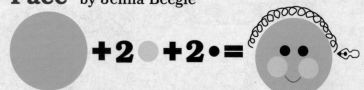

Bear by Jenna Beegle

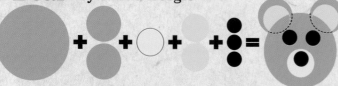

Caterpillar
by Debbie Peterson
(page 51)

Notes by Jenna Beegle

Snowman by Jenna Beegle

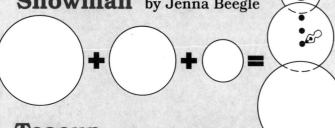

Teacup by Debbie Hewitt

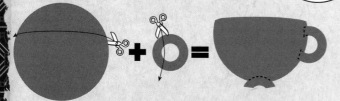

Football by Debbie Hewitt

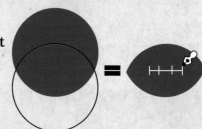

Clock by Jenna Beegle

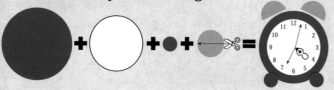

Hat by Debbie Hewitt

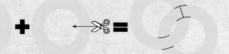

Wedding Rings by Jenna Beegle

Record by Debbie Hewitt

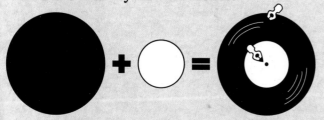

Scissors by Debbie Hewitt

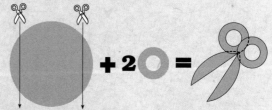

Clouds by Debbie Hewitt

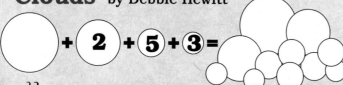

Ornament by Jenna Beegle

Beach Balls by Debbie Hewitt

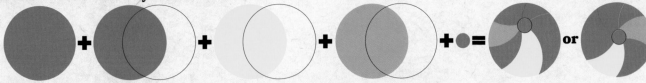

Rattle by Jenna Beegle

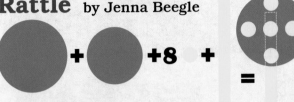

Moon by Jenna Beegle

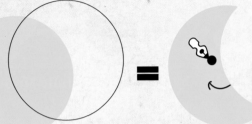

Button
by Jenna Beegle

Ribbon by Jenna Beegle

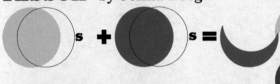

Baby Carriage by Jenna Beegle

Topiary by Jenna Beegle

Bubbles by Jenna Beegle

Make bubbles in several different sizes for a realistic look.

Paper Pizazz™: white carnations (*Floral Papers*)

Solid Paper Pizazz™: metallic gold (*Metallic Papers*), hunter green, ivory (*Solid Jewel Tones*), white (*Plain Pastels*)

Punch-Outs™: "Our Wedding Day" (*Titles*)

¼" wide circle punch: McGill, Inc.

½" wide circle punch: Marvy® Uchida

⅝" wide circle punch: Family Treasures

Corner punch: Pebbles Inc.

Gold pen: DecoColor™ by Marvy® Uchida

Decorative scissors: provincial, corkscrew by Fiskars®, Inc.

Page designer: Terri Carter for Paper Hearts

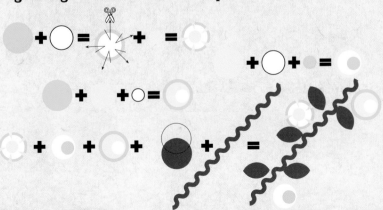

33

Heart Punches

Bunnies by Debbie Peterson (page 25)

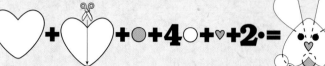

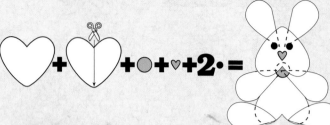

Frog by Debbie Peterson (page 98)

Butterfly by Jenna Beegle

Turkey by CJ Wilson & Julie McGuffee

Dragonfly by Susan Cobb

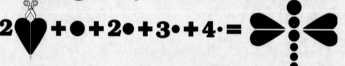

Fish by Jenna Beegle

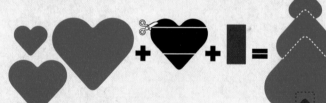

Santa by Anne-Marie Spencer

Topiary by Anne-Marie Spencer

Apple by Debbie Peterson (page 51)

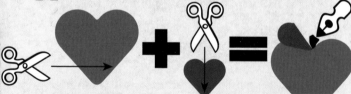

Apple by Debbie Hewitt

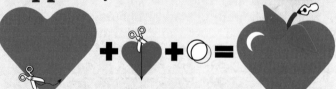

Strawberry by Debbie Hewitt

Ivy by Jenna Beegle

Shamrock
by Debbie Hewitt

Pepper by Jenna Beegle

Carrot by Debbie Hewitt

Dogwood Flower
by Debbie Hewitt

Christmas Tree
by Jenna Beegle

Streamed Heart
by Debbie Peterson (page 50)

Candy Cane
by Jenna Beegle

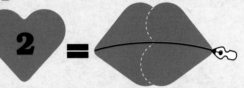

Heart Balloon
by Jenna Beegle

Mitten   by Debbie Hewitt

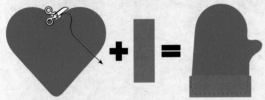

Lips   by Debbie Hewitt

Sunglasses   by Debbie Hewitt

Baby Bootie   by Debbie Hewitt

Bikini   by Debbie Hewitt

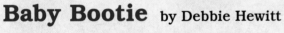

Paper Pizazz™: white carnations, delphiniums, bright ferns, ivy (*Floral Papers*), purple hydrangeas, purple swirl (*Pretty Papers*), pink hydrangeas (*Romantic Papers*)
Solid Paper Pizazz™: ivory, lavender, pink (*Plain Pastels*), purple (*Solid Jewel Tones*)
⅜" **wide heart and** 1⅜" **wide flower punches:** McGill, Inc.
Page designer: Anne-Marie Spencer for Hot Off The Press

Laurence and Anne-Marie

Star Punches

Cat Face by Jenna Beegle

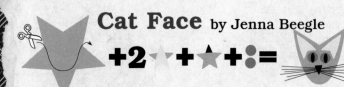

Mouse Face by Jenna Beegle

Bunny by Susan Cobb

Moth by Susan Cobb

Baby Doll by Susan Cobb

Ice Cream Cone
by Jenna Beegle

Flower by Jenna Beegle

Flower by Susan Cobb

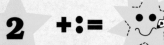

Sailboat by Susan Cobb

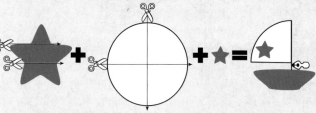

Traffic Signal by Susan Cobb

Lilypad by Susan Cobb

Starfish by Jenna Beegle

Sheriff's Badge
by Jenna Beegle

Party Hat
by Jenna Beegle

Sun by Jenna Beegle

Fireworks by Jenna Beegle

Reindeer by Susan Cobb

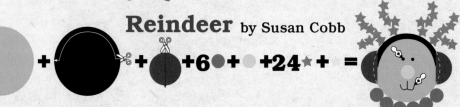

Decorated Tree
by Jenna Beegle & Susan Cobb

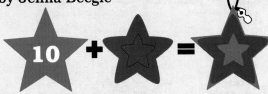 =

Crown by Susan Cobb

Star Ornament
by Jenna Beegle

10 + =

Gingerbread Boy by Susan Cobb

Star Garland by Jenna Beegle

s + s + s =

Wreath by Susan Cobb

12 + 2 + 12 =

Star Santa by Susan Cobb

+ ○ + + + + =

Snowflake
by Susan Cobb

7 + 7 + 43 =

Paper Pizazz™: burgundy tri-dot, green with stars, green checks, navy checks, navy pinstripes, burgundy pinstripes (*Dots, Checks, Plaids & Stripes*)

Solid Paper Pizazz™: white (*Solid Pastel Papers*)

½" wide star, ⅞" and 1¼" wide heart punches: Family Treasures

¼" and ½" wide circle punches: Marvy® Uchida

Alphabet stickers: Making Memories

Decorative scissors: deckle by Family Treasures

Red, green and blue pens: Zig™ Writer by EK Success, Ltd.

Page designer: Debbie Peterson

-Chad-messy

but... cute!

 + + 2 =

37

Balloon Punches

Apple by Jenna Beegle

Eggplant by Jenna Beegle

Pumpkin by Jenna Beegle

Tomato
by Susan Cobb

Strawberry by Susan Cobb

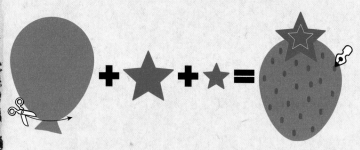

Jellybeans by Jenna Beegle

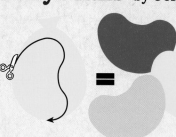

Cut many jellybeans from a variety of bright solid-color papers.

Turkey by Jenna Beegle

Turkey Dinner by Susan Cobb

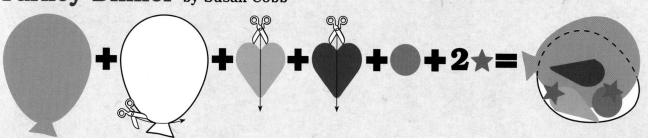

38

Flagstone Path by Jenna Beegle

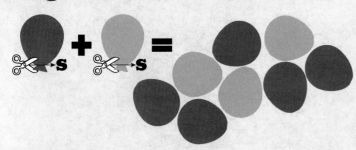

Beehive
by Jenna Beegle

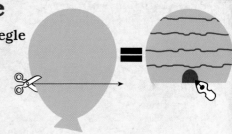

Dogwood by Susan Cobb

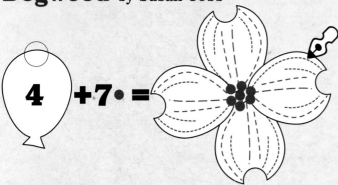

Easter Eggs by Jenna Beegle

Use a variety of pastel patterned papers to cut a basketful of colorful eggs!

Pine Cone
by Jenna Beegle

Daisy by Jenna Beegle

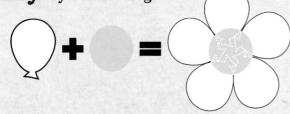

Paper Pizazz™: red lines & dots, blue chalky, bright interlock (*Bright Great Backgrounds*)
Solid Paper Pizazz™: cream, peach (*Plain Pastels*), red (*Plain Brights*), black (*Solid Jewel Tones*)
¼" wide circle, ¾" and 1¼" wide hearts punches: McGill, Inc.
⅝" wide circle, ½" wide balloon and bow punches: Marvy® Uchida
Red pen: Zig® Writer by EK Success Ltd.
Decorative scissors: scallop, ripple by Fiskars®, Inc.
Page designer: Debbie Peterson

39

Holly by Jenna Beegle

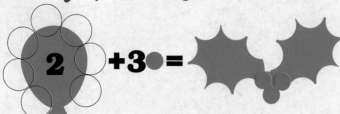

Christmas Lights by Jenna Beegle

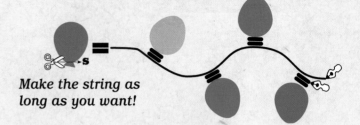

Make the string as long as you want!

Light Bulb by Susan Cobb

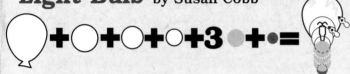

Hand Mirror by Susan Cobb

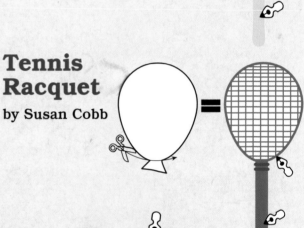

Hot Air Balloon by Susan Cobb

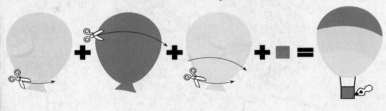

Tennis Racquet by Susan Cobb

Hot Air Balloon by Jenna Beegle

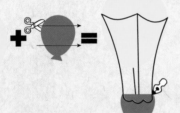

Sunglasses by Susan Cobb

Humpty Dumpty by Jenna Beegle

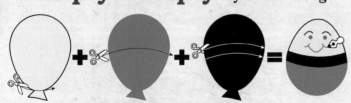

Earmuffs by Jenna Beegle

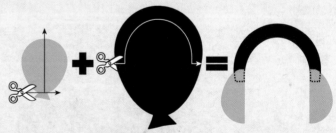

Lute by Susan Cobb

Teapot by Jenna Beegle

Froggy by Jenna Beegle

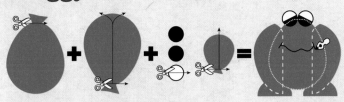

Fish by Susan Cobb

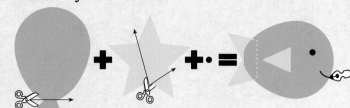

Turtle by Jenna Beegle

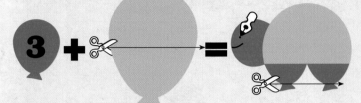

Pawprint by Jenna Beegle

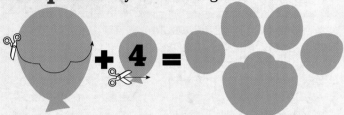

Bunny by Jenna Beegle

Mouse by Jenna Beegle

Spider by Jenna Beegle

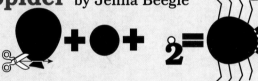

Butterfly by Susan Cobb

Octopus by Jenna Beegle

Hedgehog by Jenna Beegle

Horseshoe by Jenna Beegle

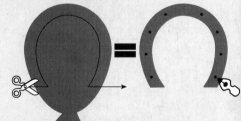

Ducky by Susan Cobb

Penguin by Jenna Beegle & Susan Cobb

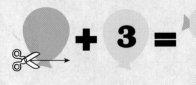

Caterpillar by Susan Cobb

41

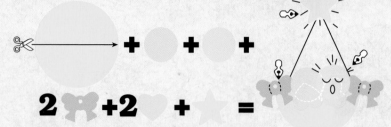

Paper Pizazz™: pastel lines, pastel dots, baby blocks (*Baby*)
Solid Paper Pizazz™: pink, yellow, blue, peach (*Plain Pastels*)
½" wide circle, ½" wide star, ⅜" wide heart and
   corner frame punches: Family Treasures
Bow punch: Marvy® Uchida
Alphabet stickers: Frances Meyer, Inc.®
Wave edge ruler: Déjà Views by C-Thru® Ruler Co.
Decorative scissors: deckle, mini pinking by Fiskars®, Inc.
Page designer: Debbie Peterson

Paper Pizazz™: clouds (*Vacation*), red & white stripes
   (*Ho Ho Ho!!!*)
Solid Paper Pizazz™: light blue, red, yellow (*Plain Brights*),
   white (*Plain Pastels*), black (*Solid Jewel Tones*)
⅜" wide heart, boat, tropical fish, sun, rectangle and spiral
   punches: Family Treasures
Red pen: Zig™ Writer by EK Success, Ltd.
Decorative scissors: heartstrings by Fiskars®, Inc.
Page designer: Anne-Marie Spencer for Hot Off The Press

Paper Pizazz™: pastel hearts (*Baby*), pastel stripes on blue
   (*Light Great Backgrounds*)
Solid Paper Pizazz™: pastel yellow, mint, pastel blue, white
   (*Plain Pastels*)
½", 1½" wide hearts, ⅛", ½", 1" wide circles, cloud, film strip,
   and bear punches: Family Treasures
Decorative scissors: deckle, zipper by Fiskars®, Inc.
Page designer: Debbie Peterson

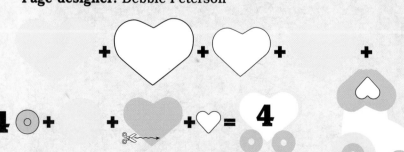

Paper Pizazz™: navy pinstripes, navy checks (*Dots, Checks, Plaids & Stripes*)
Solid Paper Pizazz™: white (*Plain Pastels*), navy (*Solid Jewel Tones*), red (*Plain Brights*)
½" wide circle punch: Fiskars®, Inc.
Leaf, sun and corner punches: Family Treasures
Alphabet stickers: ©Mrs. Grossman's Paper Co.
Decorative scissors: deckle by Fiskars®, Inc.
Red and blue pens: Zig® Writer by EK Success Ltd.
Page designer: Debbie Peterson

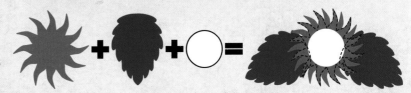

Mix plain and patterned papers with punches to create a fun frame around photos! Cut 1" wide paper squares, then add a punched shape to the center of each. Use punched bows to connect the squares.

Paper Pizazz™: pastel tri-dots, blue & yellow plaid, light blue lines & dots, white dots on lavender (*Dots, Checks, Plaids & Stripes*)
Solid Paper Pizazz™: white, yellow (*Plain Pastels*)
1¼" wide circle, spiral and heart silhouette punches: McGill, Inc.
Bear and bow punches: Marvy® Uchida
Alphabet stickers: Making Memories™
Blue pen: Zig® Writer by EK Success Ltd.
Decorative scissors: scallop, ripple by Fiskars®, Inc.
Page designer: Debbie Peterson

Paper Pizazz™: tri-dots on navy, navy checks, burgundy tri-dots (*Dots, Checks, Plaids & Stripes*)
Solid Paper Pizazz™: white, pink (*Plain Pastels*), navy, gray (*Solid Jewel Tones*)
⅝", ½" wide circles and spiral punches: Family Treasures
¼" wide circle punch: Marvy® Uchida
Alphabet stickers: Making Memories™
Corner border arch: Keeping Memories Alive™
Page designer: Debbie Peterson

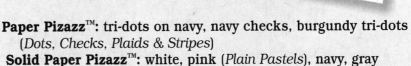

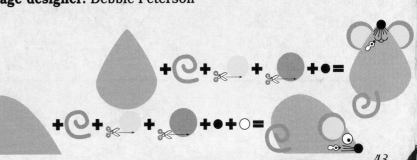

Ashton
waiting for
the parade...

Lines, Curves, Dots & Squiggles

Hand-drawn embellishments provide a unique way to give your pages a personal touch. No two designs will ever look alike! Pen work also offers great freedom of design. It allows you to create large swirls or tight curls, straight lines or stitch marks—anything you feel as you're designing your pages. And, if you make a bit of a mistake, you can simply incorporate it into your design by repeating the tiny flaw!

Often, pen work connects other elements on the page keeping them from seeming simply "stuck there." This sense of unity is shown in the examples on page 51. Drawn borders are a great way to add focus to your page design. You can border the photos or the whole page. Photo borders can be drawn on or around the mats as shown on page 47. Page borders can be as elaborate (top of page 53), or as simple (bottom of page 52) as you like! Lines might echo a scissor cut like that on page 48, or show movement such as at the top of page 49. Random dots and squiggles can also provide a festive feeling as shown on page 55!

We've provided a variety of line ideas at the tops of pages 46, 48 and 54 to inspire you. Practice with them on plain paper till you feel comfortable making each one. Then, as you get better at it, make up some of your own! Our suggestions are by no means all there are! Throughout this chapter you'll see these and many other lines, curves, dots and squiggles used in terrific ways to create simply wonderful scrapbook pages!

This chapter's background paper is from *Paper Pizazz™ Dots, Checks, Plaids & Stripes*

Basic Embellished Lines

These straight lines work well as page borders, around mats or between photos. The idea is simple—make a line, then an embellishment. It can be another line, dot, circle, heart or any combination thereof. The examples on this page are only a few ideas; you can combine these ideas, add embellishments or use several colors.

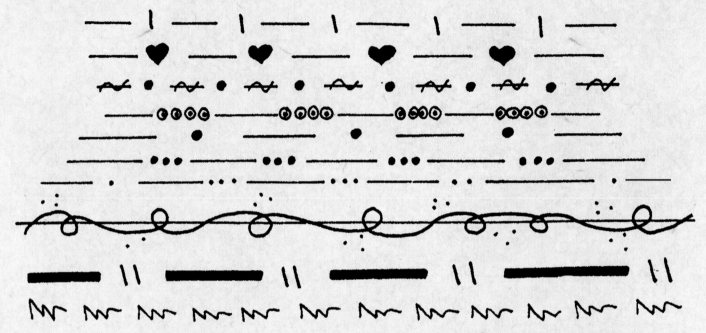

The simple —— • • • —— line around the page corrals the elements and ties the page together. The same border around the mats prevents any element from becoming disconnected. Notice the number of dots varies around the page.

Paper Pizazz™: watercolor fall leaves (*Watercolor Papers*)

Solid Paper Pizazz™: dark olive, orange (*Solid Muted Colors*)

Punch-Outs™: watercolor fall leaves (*Watercolor*)

Cardstock: 12"x12" hunter green

Decorative scissors: deckle, jumbo deckle by Family Treasures

Brown pen: Zig® Writer by EK Success Ltd.

Page designer: LeNae Gerig for Hot Off The Press

A simple — • — • border frames each element, sometimes around the matted photos and once inside the star. Mat photos on tan handmade paper with a cut in each corner. Mat again on green and add a punched star in each corner. The Fort Fearless title may look like a sticker or Punch-Out™ but it's really an enlarged photo of the sign from the actual fort!

Paper Pizazz™: barnwood (*Country*), tan handmade (*Handmade Papers*)
Solid Paper Pizazz™: hunter green, black (*Solid Jewel Tones*)
½" wide star punch: Family Treasures
Corner edger: contemporary by Fiskars®, Inc.
Gold pen: Gel Roller by Marvy® Uchida
Decorative scissors: deckle by Family Treasures
Page designer: LeNae Gerig for Hot Off The Press

The 〜〜 • 〜〜 • border surrounds the outer edge of each square mat. Connect the journaling to the border with a • on each end. The grass paper makes a great backdrop for the brightly matted photos and Punch-Out™ animal friends. The golf paper, used behind the grass and for the letters, subtly hints at the day's actions.

Paper Pizazz™: golf balls (*Sports*), grass (*Pets*)
Solid Paper Pizazz™: goldenrod, red, blue (*Plain Brights*)
Punch-Outs™: elephant, hippo, giraffes (*Photo Friends*)
Letter die cuts: Accu/Cut® Systems
Page designer: LeNae Gerig for Hot Off The Press

Curved and Multiple Lines

Adding curved lines to your page is no more work than adding straight lines—the trick is to make them look natural. If you try to be too perfect, any mistake will be noticeable; however, when you let yourself go, the "mistakes" will look like part of the design. Trust us!

When you want to be exact, such as when two lines must curve alike, use a pattern-edged ruler. They come in many different designs.

If you make a mistake, use it. Add dots or lines, or turn a bobble into a bow!

One way to use curved or multiple lines is around the border of the page. Use a white pen on a dark background. This line accents the triple matting created with patterned scissors turned in opposite directions. The Mickey & Friends letters are incorporated into the design by placing a • between each letter.

Paper Pizazz™: navy pinstripes (*Dots, Checks, Plaids & Stripes*)
Solid Paper Pizazz™: red, yellow, green, blue (*Plain Brights*)
Punch-Outs™: letters (*Disney's Mickey & Friends ABC*)
Decorative scissors: wave by Family Treasures
White pen: Zig® Opaque Writer by EK Success Ltd.
Page designer: Becky Goughnour for Hot Off The Press

Disney characters © Disney Enterprises, Inc.

48

Embellished lines can link page elements or simply enhance one area of the page. The title of this page is set off by soccer balls added to a — • — • line woven around the letters like a path. As in the golfing page on page 47, grass paper letters soften the soccer paper and brings out the deep green of the grass in the photos.

Paper Pizazz™: soccer balls (*Sports*), grass (*Pets*)
Solid Paper Pizazz™: black (*Solid Jewel Tones*), white (*Solid Pastel Papers*)
Soccer ball stickers: Stickopotamus™ by EK Success Ltd.
Letter die cuts: Accu/Cut® Systems
Decorative scissors: deckle by Family Treasures
Page designer: Becky Goughnour for Hot Off The Press

The large white mat is too bare to accent the photo properly. Watercolor pansy Punch-Outs™ are added to two corners, then a heavy mauve line on each side gives the pansies the illusion of more space. A thinner line curls around each straight line like tendrils.

Solid Paper Pizazz™: burgundy (*Solid Jewel Tones*), pale lavender (*Solid Muted Colors*), white (*Plain Pastels*)
Punch-Outs™: watercolor pansies (*Watercolor*)
Decorative scissors: deckle by Family Treasures
Mauve pen: Zig® Writer by EK Success Ltd.
Page designer: Amberly Beck

The swirled lines extending up each side of the photos are decorated with punched hearts. This continues the garden theme established by the Punch-Out™ designs. The borders at the bottom of each photo really accent the photos for a nice look.

Paper Pizazz™: white dot on black (*Stripes, Checks & Dots*)
Solid Paper Pizazz™: red, yellow (*Plain Brights*)
Punch-Outs™: suns, borders, "May", gardening girl (*Sweet Companions*)
¼" wide heart punch: Family Treasures
Page designer: LeNae Gerig for Hot Off The Press

Use lines to connect elements like the hearts and lettering on these pages. Draw the swirled lines with a blue pen, then draw small loops in red. Multi-colored dots simulate confetti or fireworks. (Streamed heart punch pattern on page 35.)

Paper Pizazz™: burgundy with stars, burgundy hearts, navy checks, navy pinstripes (*Dots, Checks, Plaids & Stripes*)

Solid Paper Pizazz™: white (*Solid Pastel Papers*), navy (*Solid Jewel Tones*)

½" wide star, 1¼", 1¾" and 2" wide heart punches: Family Treasures

Alphabet stickers: ©Mrs. Grossman's Paper Company

Decorative scissors: deckle, spindle by Fiskars®, Inc.

Heart template: Extra Special Products

Red and blue pens: Zig® Writers by EK Success Ltd.

Page designer: Debbie Peterson

Licorice (the company cat at Hot Off The Press) reigns supreme over all. This page combines several embellishment techniques: the line around the photos tied with a bow works as a mat, while the curlicue swirls, tri dots and heart strings fill the empty areas. A line "tied" with a bow connects each matted punch.

Paper Pizazz™: muted roses (*Wedding*)

Solid Paper Pizazz™: pale pink (*Solid Pastel Papers*), pink, goldenrod (*Plain Pastels*), black (*Solid Jewel Tones*)

½" wide heart, 1⅜" wide circle and cat silhouette punches: McGill, Inc.

Photo corners: Fiskars®, Inc.

Page designer: LeNae Gerig for Hot Off The Press

Patterned rulers have a great variety of edges. Draw curves to decorate the top and right page edges, then use the same ruler to cut two strips from the red with dots paper. Placing it on the green with dots paper, which has a similar pattern, gives the design an interlocking effect. To make the apples, use a template to cut red paper hearts, then trim the bottoms flat; repeat with small heart punches and punch leaves for both sizes. Use patterned scissors to cut bites from the upper and lower apples. The hungry caterpillars are overlapped punched circles. (Apple punch pattern on page 34; caterpillar punch pattern on page 32.)

Paper Pizazz™: red with dots, green with dots (*Bright Great Backgrounds*)
Solid Paper Pizazz™: red (*Plain Brights*), olive (*Solid Muted Colors*)
½" wide heart, ¼" long teardrop, ½" wide circle and leaf punches: Family Treasures
Wave edge ruler: Déjà Views by C-Thru® Ruler Co.
Heart template: Extra Special Products
Decorative scissors: deckle, scallop by Fiskars®, Inc.
Brown pen: Zig® Writer by EK Success Ltd.
Page designer: Debbie Peterson

This combination of red, white, and blue papers accents the Independence Day theme. The other elements, such as the star and flower clusters joined with a swirled lined, enhance the photo instead of competing for the viewer's attention.

Paper Pizazz™: navy checks, burgundy tri-dot (*Dots, Checks, Plaids & Stripes*)
Solid Paper Pizazz™: navy, red (*Solid Jewel Tones*), yellow (*Plain Brights*), white (*Plain Pastels*)
½" wide star, ⁵⁄₁₆" wide circle, and 1" wide flower punches: Family Treasures
White pen: Gel Roller by Marvy® Uchida
Page designer: LeNae Gerig for Hot Off The Press

Large curved lines can be really striking; however, attempting them for the first time may be a little intimidating. Practice on a blank piece of paper several times with the pen you plan to use to get the hang of it, then draw the shape on the paper with a pencil to get it just right before drawing it with a pen. Use a thin gold pen to outline the purple mat and journaling oval, then use a thicker pen for the date and swirls.

Paper Pizazz™: white rose buds (*Romantic Papers*), mauve handmade, purple handmade, green handmade (*Handmade Look Papers*)
Solid Paper Pizazz™: metallic gold (*Metallic Papers*)
Decorative scissors: jumbo classic wave by Family Treasures
Gold pens: DecoColor™ by Marvy® Uchida
Page designer: Katie Hacker for Hot Off The Press

It seems difficult to believe that anything could improve upon these photos, yet the added details do improve the page! The combination of colors and mat thicknesses makes a really lovely effect. Draw an edge that pulls the eye inward by using two different pen thicknesses, then fill the empty areas with swirls and punches. Notice that the color of the balloon picks up a mat color, while the drawn "string" accents the other details.

Paper Pizazz™: navy tiles (*Bulk Papers*)
Solid Paper Pizazz™: red, goldenrod, light blue, dark blue (*Plain Brights*), white (*Solid Pastel Papers*)
Jumbo bear and small balloon punches: Marvy® Uchida
Decorative scissors: deckle by Fiskars®, Inc.
Black pens: Artist and LePlume™ by Marvy® Uchida
Page designer: Becky Goughnour for Hot Off The Press

• punch a red and goldenrod bear
• cut the head, hands and legs off the red bear
• glue the red shirt to the bear
• draw the eyes and nose

Borders can be quick or elaborate. This one looks intricate, but is really quite easy and requires just a little more time. Sketch the long lines, varying the distance between them, then draw smaller curved lines between each row to make the webbing. Cut shells and starfish from patterned papers and add them, along with the cutouts, to the net. (Lobster pattern on page 141.)

Paper Pizazz™: oatmeal handmade (*Handmade Look Papers*), **shells** (*Vacation*), **seashells** (*Embossed Papers*) **sailboats** (*Quick & Easy*)
Solid Paper Pizazz™: blue, rust (*Solid Jewel Tones*)
Cutouts: anchor, "1989", ship's wheel (*Quick & Easy*)
Decorative scissors: wave by Family Treasures
Page designer: Sally Clarke

Seashells   Shells

Use one sheet of patterned paper to make two album pages. Cut 1⅛" wide strips of candy corn paper, glue to the page, then draw curved lines between the strips and make groups of 1–3 dots on the lines. The curves relieve the straight lines of the background. (Pumpkin patterns on page 140; candy corn pattern on page 141.)

Paper Pizazz™: candy corn (*Holidays & Seasons*)
Solid Paper Pizazz™: orange, light orange, yellow, green (*Plain Brights*), white (*Plain Pastels*), black (*Solid Jewel Tones*)
Punch-Outs™: ghosts, bat, cat, bag (*Holidays & Seasons*)
Orange and green pens: Zig® Writers by EK Success Ltd.
Page designer: Amberly Beck

Doodles, Dots & Dashes

You can do more to decorate your pages than just draw fancy lines. A little constructive doodling around the edges of a page could form a unique border. Or draw random figures in empty areas to make a background.

Take advantage of heritage photos with decorative borders; this 1935 photo came with the border shown. You can reproduce the design by drawing two outside lines filled with squiggles. For a great finish cut four corners, then draw a curvy line on each. Place the photo closer to the top of the page to leave room for the matted journaling rectangle.

Paper Pizazz™: brown plaid (*Great Outdoors*), crushed suede (*Black & White Photos*)
Solid Paper Pizazz™: orange, sienna (*Solid Muted Colors*), black (*Solid Jewel Tones*)
Decorative scissors: ripple by Fiskars®, Inc.
Black pen: LePlume™ by Marvy® Uchida
Page designer: Katie Hacker for Hot Off The Press

© & ™ Accu/Cut® Systems

Red and green papers don't have to be reserved for Christmas—adding yellow turns them into a school page! Squiggled lines, dots and punched leaves make an outstanding embellishment for these photos. It's a great, easy-to-do technique and it's simple to substitute punches hearts, stars or small stickers for the leaves to create a different theme.

Paper Pizazz™: red tri-dots (*Bulk Papers*), green with stars (*Dots, Checks, Plaids & Stripes*)
Solid Paper Pizazz™: red, green, light green (*Solid Jewel Tones*), ivory (*Solid Pastels Papers*)
Cardstock: 12"x12" ivory
Leaf punch: Family Treasures
Apple die cut: Accu/Cut® Systems
Alphabet stickers: Making Memories™
Page designer: LeNae Gerig for Hot Off The Press

Doodles, dots and dashes can form a fun background when they use colors from the matting papers. Use a ruler to draw three large offset squares around the outer edge of the white paper as shown. Place the matted photos on the page with the journaling star in the center, then draw triangles with dots, swirls and dotted lines in the empty areas. Use the silver pen for all dotted lines on the background, then draw a similar border around the star and the yellow mats.

Paper Pizazz™: navy checks, navy pin-stripes, burgundy tri-dot (*Dots, Checks, Plaids & Stripes*)

Solid Paper Pizazz™: white (*Solid Pastel Papers*), yellow (*Plain Brights*)

Yellow, blue and red pens: Zig® Writers by EK Success Ltd.

Silver pen: DecoColor™ by Marvy® Uchida

Page designer: Stephanie Taylor

The drawn gold embellishments on the center paper mimic the highly stylized title. The 3½" wide patterned paper strips on each side highlight the title. Die cuts from gold paper link the various page elements.

Paper Pizazz™: blue swirl (*Great Backgrounds*)

Solid Paper Pizazz™: metallic gold (*Metallic Papers*), purple (*Solid Jewel Tones*)

Cardstock: 12"x12" navy

Fleur de lis and star die cuts: Accu/Cut® Systems

Decorative scissors: canyon cutters, ripply, pompeii by McGill, Inc.

Gold pen: DecoColor™ by Marvy® Uchida

Page designer: LeNae Gerig for Hot Off The Press

Hanging By A Thread

Hanging punches, stickers, die cuts or drawn items adds a charming touch to any page. This technique can fill empty areas or become the focus of the page.

The "hanging" stars inspire other details, such as the moon and the words "Twinkle... Twinkle" above the photo. What may have begun as an attempt to fill the empty areas ends up as a whimsical and touching themed page. (Moon pattern on page 138.)

Paper Pizazz™: pastel stripes, pastel quilt (*Baby*)
Solid Paper Pizazz™: pink, yellow, goldenrod (*Plain Brights*)
Cardstock: 12"x12" blue
1", ½" wide stars, ½" wide circle sun punches: Marvy® Uchida
White pen: Zig® Opaque Writer by EK Success Ltd.
Page designer: LeNae Gerig for Hot Off The Press

This page makes interesting use of space; there is a distinct background and foreground, as well as a ground and sky. The effect of "falling" snow is created by keeping the upper portion of the oval bare with the photos clustered around the bottom. Punches of two sizes and colors create a two-dimensional effect. The curved lines, which "hold" the snowflakes, mimic the soft and random fall of real snowflakes.

Paper Pizazz™: snowflakes (*Christmas*), **blue** handmade (*Light Great Backgrounds*)
Solid Paper Pizazz™: blue, light blue, white (*Plain Pastels*)
Snowflake punches: Family Treasures
Decorative scissors: leaf by Fiskars®, Inc.
Blue pen: Zig® Writer by EK Success Ltd.
Page designer: Katie Hacker for Hot Off The Press

After cutting the house from the paper and inserting photos into the openings, write the title with a black pen and color in if desired. When the basic page is finished, fill the empty areas with dangling spiders—large dots with four small lines on each side.

Paper Pizazz™: haunted house (*Holidays & Seasons*)
Solid Paper Pizazz™: orange (*Plain Brights*)
Red and black pens: Zig® Writers by EK Success Ltd.
Page designer: Katie Hacker for Hot Off The Press

Create the snow-covered trees by cutting a green and a white tree. Trim the top of the white tree and glue it over the green tree. Use the mittens to connect the title with the other page elements. Turn the cloudy sky into a snowy sky by using the white pen to draw snowflakes in the empty areas.

Paper Pizazz™: clouds (*Vacation*)
Solid Paper Pizazz™: hunter green, dark blue (*Solid Jewel Tones*), red (*Plain Brights*), white (*Plain Pastels*)
Punch-Outs™: "Snow Day" (*Titles*)
Mitten stickers: Frances Meyer, Inc.®
Tree die cut: Ellison® Craft & Design
Decorative scissors: ripple by Fiskars®, Inc.
Blue pen: Zig® Writer by EK Success Ltd.
White pen: Zig® Opaque by EK Success Ltd.
Page designer: Katie Hacker for Hot Off The Press

Dress Up Your ABCs

Let's talk about journaling. What? You say you hate your handwriting? Then this chapter will offer some creative ways to use stickers, stencils, die cuts or Punch-Outs™ for journaling. And yes, we've offered two lettering styles on page 65, too.

Alphabet stickers are a convenient way to journal a name or date on your pages. Add highlights around each letter like those in the center of page 62, or embellish the journaling with other theme-related stickers as was done in the center of page 69.

You might choose to use letter templates or stencils. There are many lettering styles to choose from so you can match your theme design. Just look at the creative things the designers did with letter stencils on page 66!

Die cuts also come in letter styles, too! Some are pre-cut, or you can have the store cut them from paper you provide. The journaled name on the page at the bottom of page 61 uses die cut letters and theme-related paper. What a great effect!

Alphabet Punch-Outs™ are an easy solution for journaling. You can move them around to find just the right placement before gluing them to your page. As you can see from the examples on page 60 they provide a great finishing touch to your page.

Most styles of alphabet journaling work well when embellished. Add stickers that go with the theme of the design like on page 67. You can turn each letter a bit for fun (page 63), or keep them all in a row as shown at the top of page 69. Punch each letter and then mat them, or glue punches on top of the letters! These ideas are shown on page 70. Another idea is to cut letters from photos and use them to journal such as the examples on page 61.

There are so many fun things you can do with a name, a date or a phrase. Use your photos to spur your imagination and let the alphabet speak for you when you tell your photo's story!

This chapter's background paper is from *Paper Pizazz*™ *Stripes, Checks & Dots.*

Pretty ABC Punch-Outs™ come in silver, gold, red, blue and yellow guaranteeing you'll be able to use at least one with most papers. Silver letters spelling "TRUE LOVE" arch above and below the cropped photo on a purple delphinium background. Plain lavender paper contrasts the darker purples and separates the layers. Add silver tri-dots to the purple moiré paper and connect the letters with black swirls enhanced by white and silver.

Paper Pizazz™: purple moiré (*Pretty Papers*), delphinium (*Blooming Blossoms*)
Solid Paper Pizazz™: lavender (*Plain Pastels*)
Punch-Outs™: silver letters (*Pretty ABC*)
Purple pen: Zig® Writer by EK Success Ltd.
White pen: Zig® Opaque Writer by EK Success Ltd.
Silver pen: DecoColor™ Marvy® Uchida
Page designer: LeNae Gerig for Hot Off The Press

Set off titling in order to give it maximum impact. The elaborately layered strip, echoed in the photo's matting, separates "SARAH" from the rest of the page. Cut a ¾" wide red moiré strip with decorative scissors. Place it on a 1½" green pinstripe strip matted on gold. Triple mat, ending with gold paper cut in the "opposite" direction. Trim the strip at the top and bottom, then add the gold letters.

Paper Pizazz™: holly (*Ho Ho Ho!!!*), red moiré (*Black & White Photos*), green pinstripe, red with stars (*Dots, Checks, Plaids & Stripes*),
Solid Paper Pizazz™: metallic gold (*Metallic Papers*), green (*Solid Jewel Tones*)
Punch-Outs™: Alphabet (*Pretty ABC*)
Decorative scissors: cloud by Fiskars®, Inc.
Gold pen: Zig® Opaque Writer by EK Success Ltd.
Page Designer: Anne-Marie Spencer for Hot Off The Press

People photos are the most interesting and they are the ones you really want on your pages; however, we still take lots of scenic photos. One use for extra scenic photos is to cut them into letters, then mat on plain papers. Add strips to make them more noticeable, then date the page in the lower left corner.

Paper Pizazz™: shells on sand (*Our Vacations*), oatmeal handmade (*Handmade Papers*)

Solid Paper Pizazz™: light orange, orange, blue, green, pink (*Plain Brights*)

Ocean life stickers: ©Mrs. Grossman's Paper Company

Decorative scissors: bat wings by Fiskars®, Inc.

Page Designer: Katie Hacker for Hot Off The Press

Start a page with a black and white background paper, then add a colorful paper with an irregular floral pattern for a garden look. Great photos and stylized bumble bee Punch-Outs™ finish off the look. One other detail—Ari's name is cut from a photo of a yellow daisy field. It goes perfectly with the daisy paper!

Paper Pizazz™: black checks (*Stripes, Checks & Dots*), yellow daisies (*Floral Papers*)

Solid Paper Pizazz™: black (*Solid Jewel Tones*)

Punch-Outs™: bumble bees (*Cheerful & Charming*)

Letter die cuts: Accu/Cut® Systems

Page designer: LeNae Gerig for Hot Off The Press

"Seattle" says it all—a great example of effective and brief titling. These photos, taken at famous landmarks, really don't need a lot of embellishment. The stickers come in geometric patterns; choose papers that use the same sort of patterns to mat each photo. The matting and journaling papers are really effective next to the blue spirals paper with drawn doodles.

Paper Pizazz™: blue large spirals (*Great Backgrounds*), navy tri dot, burgundy stripes (*Dots, Checks, Plaids & Stripes*)
Letter stickers: Making Memories™
Blue pen: Zig® Writer by EK Success Ltd.
Page designer: Katie Hacker for Hot Off The Press

Allow vivid colors, such as the red on this page, to stand out by placing them on a white background and keeping the accompanying details small. The black outline to the left of each letter is a quick and easy way to enhance the stickers. Make the beach scene by irregularly cutting two 8"x1" tan handmade paper strips, then gluing the cat and mice between them as shown.

Paper Pizazz™: oatmeal handmade (*Solid Muted Colors*)
Solid Paper Pizazz™: red (*Plain Brights*)
Punch-Outs™: cat, mice (*Photo Friends*)
Alphabet stickers: Pebbles Inc.
Decorative scissors: deckle by Fiskars®, Inc.
Page Designer: Terri Carter for Paper Hearts

You don't have to show the whole football paper to get across your message! Cut a 1¾" wide strip of footballs paper and use strips of white paper to make the stripe and stitching. Mat on white, then adhere the stickers.

Paper Pizazz™: footballs, football field (*Sports*), green plaid, red tartan (*Ho Ho HO!!!*)
Solid Paper Pizazz™: white (*Plain Pastels*), black (*Solid Jewel Tones*), yellow (*Plain Brights*)
Trophy die cut: Ellison® Craft & Design
Alphabet stickers: Pebbles Inc.
Corner rounder punch: Marvy® Uchida
Page designer: Kristy Banks for Pebbles in my Pocket

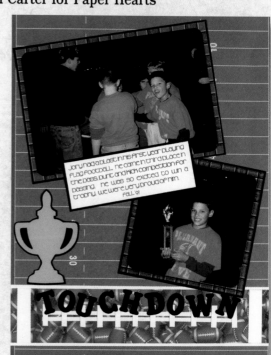

Baby blocks are a classic example of childhood; use stickers with a very defined typeface and place each on tan paper. Cut in a 1" square and mat on paper matching the stickers. Arrange askew, as if they have recently been played with, then add blocks with "A," "B" and "C" stacked at the bottom so the viewer is sure to understand the connection.

Paper Pizazz™: blocks & dots (*Child's Play*)
Solid Paper Pizazz™: green, blue, yellow, red (*Plain Brights*), tan (*Solid Muted Colors*)
Alphabet stickers: Making Memories™
Page designer: Ann Smith for Memory Lane

This page uses a similar technique to the one above, but in black and white it takes on a new element—racing! The checked flag background paper helps make the connection.

Paper Pizazz™: checkered flags (*Masculine Papers*)
Solid Paper Pizazz™: white (*Plain Pastels*), black (*Solid Jewel Tones*)
Alphabet stickers: Making Memories™
Page designer: Ann Smith for Memory Lane

By the time these large, uncropped photos are matted and placed on the page, there is not enough room for another photo. To fill the space, mat each word of the title and embellish it into a miniature scene. Stickers or punches are usually the most useful tool for this kind of work; if you can't find just the right sticker, make something with punches (see pages 28–43).

Paper Pizazz™: green with dots (*Dots, Checks, Plaids & Stripes*)
Solid Paper Pizazz™: tan, brown (*Solid Muted Colors*), green (*Plain Brights*)
Grass and alphabet stickers: ©Mrs. Grossman's Paper Company
Page designer: Ann Smith for Memory Lane

This photo has strong pink and greens, so it seems appropriate to repeat these colors on the page. Mat the photo, using colors a shade or two lighter than those in the photo. Create "Pretty In Pink" by using a circle cutter to cut perfect 1½" wide mint circles. Place a sticker in the center of each and mat on 1¾" bright pink squares. Place a 1¾" mint swirl square offset under each bright pink square. Add silver dots to all plain mint paper.

Paper Pizazz™: mint swirl (*Light Great Backgrounds*), pink moiré (*Our Wedding*)
Solid Paper Pizazz™: mint (*Plain Pastels*), pink (*Plain Brights*)
Alphabet stickers: Making Memories
Decorative scissors: ripple by Fiskars®, Inc.
Silver pen: Marvy® Uchida
Circle cutter: Fiskars®, Inc.
Page designer: Stephanie Taylor

The black, white and red papers mimic the room decor in the photo. Use a pen to draw the checks on white paper so they follow the curve of the photo. Rework the traditional sticker-block titling by cutting the blocks into geometric shapes. The shapes can follow the curve of the letter or work against it— both ways look spectacular!

Paper Pizazz™: black checks (*Stripes, Checks & Dots*)
Solid Paper Pizazz™: red (*Plain Brights*), white (*Plain Pastels*)
Solid paper: 12"x12" black
Alphabet stickers: Making Memories™
Page designer: Stephanie Taylor

This page is a collection of old and new photos tied together by their subject matter! The details, such as the camera Punch-Out™ and film strip, set the scene and the journaling makes it perfectly clear what's going on. The metallic papers bring out the best in both the black and white and the color photos. Notice the hand-lettered "A FAMILY OF PHOTO FOLKS" squares mimic the gray and white photos—even to the deckle edge!

Paper Pizazz™: metallic dots (*Metallic Papers*)
Solid Paper Pizazz™: metallic gold (*Metallic Papers*), gray (*Solid Jewel Tones*), white (*Plain Pastels*)
Punch-Outs™: camera, film strip (*Vacation*), "Strike a Pose" (*Sayings*)
Decorative scissors: deckle by Family Treasures
Page designer: Sally Clarke

This page says "party" at a glance because the big bow makes the page look like a package. Use large punches to hold your lettering; the letters look complex, but really they are stick letters with one side made thicker than the other.

Tip: This same page design would work beautifully in red and green papers for Christmas.

Paper Pizazz™: coral reef, red with dots (*Great Backgrounds*)
Solid Paper Pizazz™: yellow, green, orange, blue, dark blue (*Plain Brights*)
Balloon punch: Family Treasures
Decorative scissors: deckle by Family Treasures
Page designer: Katie Hacker for Hot Off The Press

Since details fade over time, it's important to archive them as well as your photos! For large letters, develop a stick alphabet such as the one on this page—use a ruler to draw the letters if necessary. Then use a simple style of handwriting to write around a mat. The curve of the lettering will hide your mistakes and the even width of the mat will keep your lettering about the same size.

Paper Pizazz™: barnwood (*Country*), cedar handmade (*Handmade Papers*)
Solid Paper Pizazz™: brown, yellow, green, orange (*Solid Muted Colors*)
Deckle wave scissors: Family Treasures
Page designer: Katie Hacker for Hot Off The Press

Lettering and paper strips go together like kids and fun—one is perfect for the other! Strips display the title without making it compete for attention. Then with the extra space you can add fun details. Spiral, snowflake, triangle and flower punches fill the extra space around the stamped and matted letters on this 2" wide strip. Continue the look by matting one side of the strip with a straight orange mat and use scissors to cut a red mat on the other side.

Paper Pizazz™: dots on purple (*Child's Play*)
Solid Paper Pizazz™: green, blue, red, yellow, purple (*Plain Brights*), white (*Plain Pastels*)
Snowflake, sun, triangle and flower punches: Family Treasures
Spiral punch: All Night Media®, Inc.
Letter rubber stamps: Close to My Heart
Computer typeface: Crayon by D. J. Inkers™
Decorative scissors: scallop, mini scallop by Fiskars®, Inc.
Page designer: Kristy Banks for Pebbles in my Pocket

This full spread, with its bright colors and lopsided letters looks fun! Cut each letter using a stencil and place it on a circle. Some circles are plain while some have a swirl under the letter. Notice the lavender triangles under the "CRAZY" circles. The purple dot background links both pages.

Paper Pizazz™: dots on purple (*Child's Play*)

Solid Paper Pizazz™: pale purple, white (*Plain Pastels*)

Punch-Outs™: bugs (*Cheerful & Charming*)

Alphabet stencil: Pebbles Inc.

Purple pen: Metallic Gel Roller by Marvy® Uchida

Page designer: Heather Hummel

Have some fun with your papers! Embellish barnwood paper strips with black dots to make them look like they are nailed together. Use a similar technique for "BOARDWALK" barnwood letters. Like the page above, the smaller journaling beside the photos making the viewer interested in each photo as well as the page as a whole.

Paper Pizazz™: barnwood (*Country*)

Solid Paper Pizazz™: light gray, black (*Solid Jewel Tones*), white (*Plain Pastels*)

Small foot punch: Family Treasures

Alphabet stencil: Pebbles Inc.

Decorative scissors: deckle by Fiskars®, Inc.

Page designer: Nancy Church for Pebbles in my Pocket

Every detail is linked on this page! Double mat the photo (the crayon paper is cut from the center of the background), then offset mat twice more. Crayons cut from the background paper fill the corners; add Punch-Outs™ and cutouts of crayons to the corners. Use the pattern to cut a white block, then follow the inner lines to outline each block with a pen. Place a letter in the center of each.

Paper Pizazz™: crayons (*School Days*)

Solid Paper Pizazz™: blue, green, orange, red, goldenrod (*Plain Brights*)

Punch-Outs™: crayons (*School*)

Cutouts: crayons (*School Days*)

Letter die cuts: Ellison® Craft & Design

Orange, red, blue and green pens: Zig® Writers by EK Success Ltd.

Decorative scissors: ripple by Fiskars®, Inc.

Page designer: Amberly Beck

It's clever to cut John's name out of the same football paper as the background—it links everything together. The broken lines around "JOHN" add a nice touch. Mat the photo using the team colors, then make the strip and corners using the same colors. The large football Punch-Outs™ in the corners focus the eye and direct it downward.

Paper Pizazz™: footballs (*Sports*), green with stars (*Dots, Checks, Plaids & Stripes*)
Solid Paper Pizazz™: black (*Solid Jewel Tones*), yellow (*Plain Brights*)
Punch-Outs™: football (*Kids*)
Letter die cuts: Accu/Cut® Systems
Page designer: Katie Hacker for Hot Off The Press

Here's a great way to use stickers that match your theme. These stickers interact with the letters, connecting them to the rest of the page. Place the stickers in natural positions and draw loops, dashes and dots to signal movement.

Paper Pizazz™: burgundy with stars, burgundy tri dot (*Dots, Checks, Plaids & Stripes*)
Solid Paper Pizazz™: black (*Solid Jewel Tones*), white (*Plain Pastels*)
Cheerleaders stickers: ©Mrs. Grossman's Paper Company
Decorative scissors: scallop by Fiskars®, Inc.
Red pen: Zig® Brush by EK Success Ltd.
Page designer: Katie Hacker for Hot Off The Press

Place each letter on a yellow rectangle, with ants and other bug stickers crawling over the letters like an obstacle. Cut apart a sun punch to make the grass behind the letters. Arrange the letters diagonally and use more bug stickers to fill the empty spaces.

Paper Pizazz™: grass (*Pets*), spirals on black (*Bright Great Backgrounds*)
Solid Paper Pizazz™: pale yellow (*Plain Pastels*), green (*Solid Jewel Tones*)
Alphabet stickers: Making Memories™
Bug stickers: ©Mrs. Grossman's Paper Company
Sun punch: Marvy® Uchida
Decorative scissors: mini pinking, small scallop by Fiskars®, Inc.
Page designer: Debbie Peterson

Letter stencils are relatively new in the scrapbooking market, but they're a great tool, allowing you to use the same papers as on your page if you don't have access to a die cutting machine. Like the cheerleading page, Santa hat stickers interact with the letters to reinforce the holiday theme. At the side, a journaling block tells the complete story.

Paper Pizazz™: white dot on red (*Ho Ho Ho!!!*)
Solid Paper Pizazz™: hunter green (*Solid Jewel Tones*), white (*Plain Pastels*)
Alphabet stencil: Pebbles Inc.
Holly and Santa hats stickers: ©Mrs. Grossman's Paper Company
Red and green pens: Gel Rollers by Marvy® Uchida
Page designer: Heather Hummel

What a dear photo and the journaling block is perfect— another creative use of stickers to accent lettering! The paws are hand-drawn, but they are an oval with small dots around it. Star Punch-Outs™ embellish the straight mats and complement the background paper.

Paper Pizazz™: sun & moon (*Baby*)
Solid Paper Pizazz™: blue, yellow, goldenrod (*Plain Brights*)
Punch-Outs™: stars (*Baby*)
Alphabet stickers: Déjà Views™ by C-Thru® Ruler Co.
Kitten stickers: ©Mrs. Grossman's Paper Company
Page designer: LeNae Gerig for Hot Off The Press

This page beautifully captures Josh's day in the garden! When possible, use papers that duplicate an object or theme in the photos, such as the yellow daisies paper on this page. The ivy stickers grow along Josh's name and each photo, linking them to the background paper for a nice look.

Paper Pizazz™: ivy, yellow daisies (*Blooming Blossoms*)

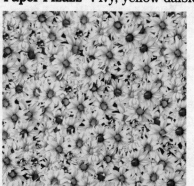

Solid Paper Pizazz™: purple, deep blue (*Solid Jewel Tones*)
Ivy leaf stickers: ©Mrs. Grossman's Paper Company
Photographs: Front Street Photo
Page designer: LeNae Gerig for Hot Off The Press

When titling letters don't take up the whole area, there are two basic approaches: center them or find something to take up the extra space! The baby buggy sticker on this page is the extra character this headline needed, while the baby stickers are fun embellishments of Katie's name.

Paper Pizazz™: pastel stripes on pink (*Great Backgrounds*), pastel dots on yellow (*Stripes, Checks & Dots*)
Solid Paper Pizazz™: yellow (*Plain Pastels*)
Letter die cuts: Accu/Cut® Systems
Baby stickers: ©Mrs. Grossman's Paper Company
Page designer: Katie Hacker for Hot Off The Press

When you need to separate letters in order to fill a space, be careful to join them. Swirly lines and dots combine these letters into a single title. Easter stickers dance around them, reinforcing the theme. Picking colors from the background paper provides lots of choices for the mats and paper strip.

Paper Pizazz™: blue & yellow plaid (*Light Great Backgrounds*)
Solid Paper Pizazz™: purple, blue, pale yellow, mint (*Plain Pastels*)
Letter and Easter stickers: ©Mrs. Grossman's Paper Company
Decorative scissors: scallop by Fiskars®, Inc.
Purple pen: Zig® Writer by EK Success Ltd.
Page designer: Katie Hacker for Hot Off The Press

Titling and journaling don't have to be in one area. This page has three different journaling areas arranged diagonally on the page. Remember, a diagonal arrangement is very interesting, especially when contrasted to equally strong horizontal or vertical elements such as the photos and plaid strips. The star stickers reinforce the diagonal and the fun of the day!

Paper Pizazz™: blue chalky (*Bright Great Backgrounds*), red & blue plaid (*Masculine Papers*)
Solid Paper Pizazz™: burgundy, dark blue (*Solid Muted Colors*), black (*Solid Jewel Tones*), blue, light blue (*Solid Bright Papers*)
Seashell and number die cuts: Accu/Cut® Systems
Star stickers: Frances Meyer®, Inc.
Page designer: Becky Goughnour for Hot Off The Press

© & ™ Accu/Cut® Systems

Bi-colored papers are very easy to work with because the simplest details finish the page beautifully. Solid blue and white mats separate the photo and letters from the background. The punched stars along Jordon and the photo play on the colors making the eye move back and forth. The cat Punch-Out™ above the photo softens the stark colors and adds an offset element.

Paper Pizazz™: navy checks (*Dots, Checks, Plaids & Stripes*)
Solid Paper Pizazz™: navy blue (*Solid Jewel Tones*), white (*Plain Pastels*)
Punch-Outs™: cat (*Photo Friends*)
¼" wide star punch: Family Treasures
Letter die cuts: Ellison® Craft & Design
Decorative scissors: mini pinking by Fiskars®, Inc.
Page designer: Shauna Wright for Paper Hearts

You might think a busy background paper will limit your embellishments. Not so—they actually add more choices! The swirl punches on "Playing" reinforce the fun and playful photos. The three Punch-Outs™ connect the photos and form a triangle that balances the photo triangle. Notice all elements on the page have a single mat to separate them from the background paper.

Paper Pizazz™: hearts, coils & stars (*Childhood Memories*)
Solid Paper Pizazz™: red, blue, yellow, orange, light orange, green, purple, dark blue (*Plain Brights*)
Punch-Outs™: bucket, ball, wagon (*Kid's*)
Letter die cuts: Accu/Cut® Systems
Swirl punch: McGill, Inc.
Decorative scissors: cork screw by Fiskars®, Inc.
Page designer: LeNae Gerig for Hot Off The Press

Masculine pages, like this one, use strong arrangements and colors rather than cute details to draw attention. Like the page before, three elements form a strong center of interest, with a strip at the top and bottom balancing them. The star punches on Mike's name work very well even though they aren't in the papers or photos, proving you can always add an extra touch.

Paper Pizazz™: forest camouflage, jeeps & transports (*Military Papers*)
Solid Paper Pizazz™: brown, hunter green, olive, tan (*Solid Muted Colors*)
¼" **wide star punch:** Family Treasures
Photo corners: Fiskars®, Inc.
Tent and letter die cuts: Accu/Cut® Systems
Decorative scissors: deckle wave by Family Treasures
Page designer: LeNae Gerig for Hot Off The Press

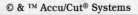

© & ™ Accu/Cut® Systems

What a lovely page! Choose an elegant background paper to start the page. The photo has five mats, The first two and last two are very narrow, while the center ivory mat is ⅜" wide. Use the filmstrip punch around the ivory edge, then weave ribbon through the holes as shown. Cut the letters from ivory paper, then repeat the punch and weaving process. Double-mat and glue the letters above and below the photo. Tie a small shoestring bow and glue to the center of each letter.

Paper Pizazz™: antique laces, purple moiré (*Pretty Papers*)
Solid Paper Pizazz™: lavender, ivory (*Plain Pastels*)
⅛" **wide lavender satin ribbon:** C.M. Offray & Son, Inc.
Filmstrip punch: Family Treasures
Alphabet die cuts: Accu/Cut® Systems
Decorative scissors: provincial by Fiskars®, Inc.
Page designer: Anne-Marie Spencer for Hot Off The Press

Mix Your Mats & Frame Your Photos

Mats and frames can help establish a focal point, develop interest and add fun to the scrapbook pages you create. They might help to convey the theme or set the mood of the page. This chapter is designed to show how you can use matting and framing techniques to create the biggest impact for your page design.

Traditionally, a mat is placed behind the photo and a frame is placed on top of or around the photo. Aside from that, there are no rules to matting or framing. Matting techniques are limited only by your imagination, and framing a photo provides just as much freedom for creativity!

A mat can be the same shape as the photo like on page 76, or a different shape to add interest like the examples on page 74. Mats can have a different shape than the photos, providing a great place for journaling (three examples of this are shown on page 77). Or mats can be embellished with punches, creating interest and fun (two examples are shown on page 78). Page 75 shows a unique way to mat silhouette cut photos. The effect is both intriguing and endearing as you can see!

Frames are a great addition to mats. Frames might be created by using punches or Punch-Outs™ as shown by the examples on page 80 (stickers or die cuts can make great frames too). You can use die cuts to frame just one photo on a page, or to frame the whole page like at the bottom of page 81. And paper-strip frames around the entire photo are a fun way to add dimension to your page as you can see from the examples on page 82.

The effects you create from mixing your mats and framing your photos are endless as this chapter shows. Let the examples here inspire you to design some of the best pages your scrapbook will include!

This chapter's background paper is from *Paper Pizazz*™ *Baby's First Year*.

Large patterns or die cuts can be fun mats! Here, oval photos fit in large mittens attached with paper string. The snowball with journaling and metallic snowflakes reinforce the snowflake patterned paper. (Mitten pattern on page 140.)

Paper Pizazz™: snowflakes (*Christmas*)
Solid Paper Pizazz™: light blue (*Plain Brights*), white (*Plain Pastels*)
Snowflake and alphabet stickers: ©Mrs. Grossman's Paper Company
Decorative scissors: colonial by Fiskars®, Inc.
Page designer: Amberly Beck

The earthy color of the oatmeal handmade creates a sandy background while the square spirals paper hints at the tropical nature of the islands. Notice the photos sit at an angle on the mats while the palm trees shelter the people in the photos. Finally, bare feet complete the theme.

Paper Pizazz™: oatmeal handmade (*Solid Muted Colors*), **square spirals** (*Bright Great Backgrounds*)
Solid Paper Pizazz™: olive, dark olive, brown, buff (*Solid Muted Colors*)
Palm tree and foot stencils: Westrim® Crafts
Foot punch: Family Treasures
Dark and light brown pens: Zig® Writer by EK Success Ltd.
Decorative scissors: spindle, deckle by Fiskars®, Inc.
Page designer: Debbie Peterson

For a great look, silhouette a photo and mat it on a different shape! Center Derek's photo on a small black oval which has a large rectangle mat. Place it on the page off-center to make room for a sticker train. Use the same scissors to cut the outer strips, connecting the train tracks (and therefore the train) to the page.

Tip: The train stickers could be replaced by dinosaurs, school items, bicycles or cars.

Paper Pizazz™: red & blue plaid (*Masculine Papers*)
Solid Paper Pizazz™: tan (*Plain Pastels*), black (*Solid Jewel Tones*)
Train stickers: ©Mrs. Grossman's Paper Company
Border punch: Family Treasures
Decorative scissors: zipper by Fiskars®, Inc.
Page designer: Debbie Peterson

This page uses two levels of matting. The entire page works as the first level; cut the daisy paper following the flowers, then glue it to a green sheet. The silhouetted photos are the second layer; glue each to a small matted oval, then place them in the center of the daisy paper.

Paper Pizazz™: white daisies (*Floral Papers*)
Solid Paper Pizazz™: hunter green (*Solid Jewel Tones*), ivory (*Plain Pastels*)
Alphabet stickers: Making Memories™
Decorative scissors: deckle by Fiskars®, Inc.
Page designer: Debbie Peterson

The corners on this page capture the eye, redirecting it to the double-matted photo. Mat each delphinium corner with green, then place a piece of laser lace over it. Glue one to each corner, adding the remaining lace between the corners.

Tip: Use the bride's colors for wedding pages.

Paper Pizazz™: delphinium (*Floral Papers*), laser lace (*Romantic Papers*), silver daisies (*Embossed Papers*)
Solid Paper Pizazz™: green, blue (*Solid Muted Colors*)
Silver pen: Zig® Writer by EK Success Ltd.
Decorative scissors: colonial by Fiskars®, Inc.
Page designer: Katie Hacker for Hot Off The Press

laser lace

Matting is like making a layer cake—the first layer is pretty, but when you're finished your eyes and your mouth water! Larger pages allow so many more layers and choices. This page uses papers along two themes— handmade and watercolor. Both paper types have so many varying colors and textures that perfectly matched colors aren't necessary.

Paper Pizazz™: mauve handmade (*Handmade Look Papers*), green handmade, purple handmade (*Handmade Papers*), purple pansies (*Watercolor Florals*)
Solid Paper Pizazz™: olive, purple, pale purple (*Solid Muted Colors*)
Punch-Outs™: purple pansies (*Watercolor*)
Decorative scissors: deckle, deckle wave by Family Treasures
Page designer: Katie Hacker for Hot Off The Press

Use mats for more than making your photo look better! Use them to hold journaling, like a caption in a magazine. Cut the mat larger on one side than the photo and use this extra area to hold the journaling. Add another mat so the journaling mat has its own matting.

Paper Pizazz™: eagles & stars (*Military Papers*)
Solid Paper Pizazz™: red, blue, goldenrod (*Plain Brights*)
Cutout: eagle (*Military Papers*)
Star punch: Family Treasures
Page designer: LeNae Gerig for Hot Off The Press

Another technique—crop the photo, then cut off one corner and mat with a narrow paper border, then add another mat or two. This technique makes a clever space for lettering.

Paper Pizazz™: painted pansies (*Watercolor Florals*)
Solid Paper Pizazz™: purple, blue, yellow (*Plain Pastels*)
Punch-Outs™: painted pansies (*Watercolor*)
Decorative scissors: jumbo lace scallop by Family Treasures
Page designer: LeNae Gerig for Hot Off The Press

Similarly, many photos have a small area of interest—sometimes right at the edge. Keep the edge flat and crop the action into a circle. Mat on a circle and journal on the extra space, instead of having to "find" a space for journaling.

Paper Pizazz™: bubbles (*Baby*)
Solid Paper Pizazz™: blue, white (*Plain Pastels*)
Punch-Outs™: duckies (*Baby*), saying (*Titles*)
Splat stickers: ©Mrs. Grossman's Paper Company
Blue pen: Zig® Writer by EK Success Ltd.
Decorative scissors: mini scallop by Fiskars®, Inc.
Page designer: Debbie Peterson

You can find punches to match so many themes. The photos suggest water, the paper suggests drops, so a teardrop punch is perfect! Punch the mat to allow the white paper to show through. Use stickers for the page title and print the journaling on a computer printer. The hose directs the eye from element to element.

Paper Pizazz™: water drops (*Child's Play*)
Solid Paper Pizazz™: silver (*Metallic Papers*), green, blue, dark blue (*Plain Brights*), white (*Plain Pastels*)
½" long teardrop punch: McGill, Inc.
Computer typeface: fiddlesticks by D.J. Inkers™
Alphabet stickers: Pebbles Inc.
Page designer: Kristy Banks for Pebbles in my Pocket

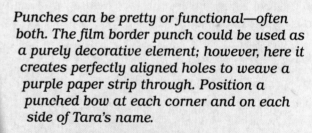

Punches can be pretty or functional—often both. The film border punch could be used as a purely decorative element; however, here it creates perfectly aligned holes to weave a purple paper strip through. Position a punched bow at each corner and on each side of Tara's name.

Paper Pizazz™: purple daisies (*Floral Papers*)
Solid Paper Pizazz™: purple (*Solid Jewel Tones*), white (*Plain Pastels*)
Film border and bow punches: Family Treasures
Decorative scissors: deckle by Fiskars®, Inc.
Page designer: Debbie Peterson

Paper Pizazz™ papers are designed to coordinate with each other and with plain papers. Pinks and oranges are the outstanding colors on the spring flowers paper, making them the obvious choice for matting. The touch of periwinkle is the perfect color for the last mat, making the photo stand out while still tying it to the other elements. Adapt stencil designs for your scrapbook pages. Trace this frame onto paper, then use an X-acto® knife to cut it out. Use a template to cut the mat into an oval.

Paper Pizazz™: spring flowers (*Watercolor Florals*)
Solid Paper Pizazz™: goldenrod, blue, pink (*Plain Pastels*)
Frame stencil: StenSource International, Inc.
Decorative scissors: Victorian by Fiskars®, Inc.
Page designer: LeNae Gerig for Hot Off The Press

Make your own custom mat! Fold a piece of white paper in quarters, place the dashed lines on the folds and trace the window. Cut out along the solid lines and unfold. Use this pattern to make the green window, then punch to let the background paper show through. Use a gold pen for the journaling—it looks really good on the dark green. (Frame pattern on page 140.)

Paper Pizazz™: yellow daisies (*Floral Papers*)
Solid Paper Pizazz™: hunter green (*Solid Muted Tones*)
Border punch: McGill, Inc.
Silver pen: Gel Roller by Marvy® Uchida
Page designer: Debbie Peterson

© & ™ Accu/Cut® Systems

Wow! You probably couldn't imagine taking the time to cut a page like this! But it's simpler than you think with some easy folding. Fold the sponged purple paper into eights, then use the bear die cut to cut the paper placed on the folds. Fold a ¾" wide purple strip and use the heart punch to make the border. Separate the two purple patterned papers with a deep purple plain paper and accent the holes in the designs with lavender.

Paper Pizazz™: purple wiggle, sponged purple (*Bright Great Backgrounds*)
Solid Paper Pizazz™: lavender, deep purple (*Solid Muted Colors*)
4-heart and bear punches: McGill, Inc.
Bear die cut: Accu/Cut® Systems
Cloud scissors: Fiskars®, Inc.
Page designer: Anne-Marie Spencer for Hot Off The Press

Punches are a great way to enhance a basic mat. Punches weave the page colors back into the photo, balance the page or simply add interest. Notice the way these punches are grouped. No group is the same size or in the same place—this balances the page and keeps the eye moving.

Paper Pizazz™: pink & blue plaid (*Dots, Checks, Plaids & Stripes*)
Solid Paper Pizazz™: blue, pink, olive, green, buff (*Solid Muted Colors*)
Flower, small circle, large and small maple leaf punches: Family Treasures
Decorative scissors: deckle, provincial by Fiskars®, Inc.
Page designer: Debbie Peterson

Create interest by placing punches in different places, angling the page elements, varying the orientation of photos (one tall, one wide) and dividing the page into distinctly separate areas.

Paper Pizazz™: blue tiles, blue chalky (*Bright Great Backgrounds*)
Solid Paper Pizazz™: dark blue, hunter green (*Solid Jewel Tones*) white (*Plain Pastels*)
½" wide circle, flower and leaf punches: Family Treasures
Blue pen: Zig® Writer by EK Success Ltd.
Decorative scissors: deckle by Family Treasures
Page designer: Debbie Peterson

Punch-Outs™ gathered around a photo make a charming frame, setting an instant theme. Choose a color scheme before beginning—this page uses red, yellow and blue with a dash of green.

Paper Pizazz™: school tartan (*School Days*)
Solid Paper Pizazz™: red, blue, yellow (*Plain Brights*)
Punch-Outs™: apples, bus, scissors, grouped crayons, single crayons, books, brush, pencil, school house (*School*), banner (*Kids*)
Page designer: LeNae Gerig for Hot Off The Press

Every part of this page works together to make a priceless image. While one mat is cut with straight scissors, the other is framed with die cuts. The mix of colors is pleasing and the contrast of the smooth mats and the bushy leaves is a visual pleasure. Another trick for adding interest—one photo slips off the page while the other is centered in the space. Finally, scatter leaves like piles waiting for someone to pounce them.

Paper Pizazz™: red plaid (*Masculine Papers*)
Solid Paper Pizazz™: light orange, blue (*Plain Brights*), deep rust, rust, olive, light olive, dark olive (*Solid Jewel Tones*)
Oak leaf die cut: Accu/Cut® Systems
Page designer: Ann Smith for Memory Lane

© & ™ Accu/Cut® Systems

Though the red roses background is beautiful, it needs a lighter contrast to have its maximum visual impact. The white roses, with their elegant green stems, are the perfect touch. They make a flawless frame around the cluster of photographs. (Rose pattern on page 141.)

Paper Pizazz™: red roses (*Blooming Blossoms*)
Solid Paper Pizazz™: metallic gold (*Metallic Papers*), hunter green (*Solid Jewel Tones*), white (*Plain Pastels*)
Rose die cut: Ellison® Craft & Design
Black calligraphy pen: Calligraphy™ by Marvy® Uchida
Decorative scissors: deckle by Family Treasures
Page designer: Becky Goughnour for Hot Off The Press

Strips of paper make some of the simplest and most striking frames. The photos were matted on black, then the purple strips were laid over the edge of the photo to make an old-fashioned frame which relates to the background paper. A photo of Brittney in costume is blown up and silhouette cropped, then glued to the lower page. This helps the viewer find her in the other photos.

Tip: the same technique works very well with brown paper and drawn lines to make it look like wood for a rustic page.

Paper Pizazz™: records (*50's & 60's Papers*)
Solid Paper Pizazz™: purple (*Plain Brights*), black (*Solid Jewel Tones*)
Page designer: LeNae Gerig for Hot Off The Press

Small spaces separate the strips around these photos, creating a triple-framing effect as the barnwood paper shows through. Because of this, the paper and the colors link the photos to the page. Use blue gingham paper heart punches and plain colored spiral punches to add color and reinforce the country theme.

Paper Pizazz™: barnwood, blue gingham (*Country*)
Solid Paper Pizazz™: brown, light brown (*Solid Muted Colors*), white (*Plain Pastels*)
⅞" wide heart and spiral punches: Family Treasures
Brown pen: Zig® Writer by EK Success Ltd.
Page designer: Debbie Peterson

1. **For pressure embossing:** Lay a piece of tape on your clothes a few times and pull it off, then tape the stencil on the paper.
2. Flip the paper over; place on a light source (window or light box). Trace the stencil outline with an embossing tool or stylus.

If you want to preserve a photo without cropping it, place an embossed mat (buy it or use the directions above to make an embossed framing using a stencil) over the photo. Go over the embossing with a colored pencil. The peach pencil used here and a thin mat added to the inner oval tie the mat to the outer page with its offset, check mat.

Paper Pizazz™: peach stripes, mint checks (*Stripes, Dots & Checks*), mint tri-dots (*Light Great Backgrounds*)
Solid Paper Pizazz™: white (*Plain Pastels*)
Embossed mat: Making Memories™
Peach colored pencil: EK Success Ltd.
Page designer: LeNae Gerig for Hot Off The Press

When you have a lot of photos of a particular event and person, create a "character study" page. Use ½" wide strips to divide the page into many 3½" sections. Journal the center square, then place a matted circular photo in each remaining piece. Finally, use Punch-Outs™ to embellish and connect the photos.

Paper Pizazz™: white dot on red, Christmas candy (*Christmas Time*)
Solid Paper Pizazz™: red (*Plain Brights*)
Punch-Outs™: candy, candy canes (*Christmas*)
White pen: Zig® Opaque Writer by EK Success Ltd.
Red and green pens: Zig® Millennium by EK Success Ltd.
Decorative scissors: ripply by McGill, Inc.
Page designer: LeNae Gerig for Hot Off The Press

By using one common element, you can link a page together like a pro. The black and white border, paper and stamps on this page connect each element. The mats really stand out because they are the widest paper on the page, repeating the black and white border. Notice the wonderful use of mixed mats: the oval photo of Madison in a rectangular mat, then the heart inside a circular mat. Stamp the bows on white paper, cut out and add to embellish.

Paper Pizazz™: peach with suns (*Janie Dawson's Sweet Companions*), black checks, blue tri-dot (*Dots, Checks, Plaids & Stripes*)
Solid Paper Pizazz™: white, green, blue, pink, goldenrod (*Plain Pastels*)
Bow rubber stamp: Rubber Stampede®
¼" and ⅜" wide star punches: Family Treasures
Black calligraphy pen: Calligraphy™ by Marvy® Uchida
Photographs: Allison Photography
Page designer: Becky Goughnour for Hot Off The Press

The clouds on this page aren't exactly frames—they don't surround the photo. However, they do accent the photos, achieving the same purpose. The corners frame the page, defining page edges and focusing the eye.

Paper Pizazz™: sun & moon (*Childhood*), clouds (*Vacation*)
Solid Paper Pizazz™: yellow, white (*Plain Pastels*), dark blue (*Plain Brights*)
½" wide star and bow punches: Marvy® Uchida
Corner edger: Keeping Memories Alive™
Dark blue pen: Zig® Writer by EK Success Ltd.
Page designer: Debbie Peterson

Were you planning to do anything with those extra pieces of paper? The ones that are just too pretty to throw away? Trim them into 3" long pieces of varying widths and arrange them around the photo to make a unique mat—like a painting palette filled with different shades of the same color.

Paper Pizazz™: pink & purple plaid, pastel dots, white dots on lavender (*Dots, Checks, Plaids & Stripes*), bachelor's buttons (*Floral Papers*)
Solid Paper Pizazz™: deep purple, lavender (*Solid Muted Colors*)
Basket, bow and flower stickers: ©Mrs. Grossman's Paper Company
Corner slot punch: Family Treasures
Alphabet stickers: Francis Meyer, Inc.®
Decorative scissors: Victorian by Fiskars®, Inc.
Page designer: Amberly Beck

Because the rose wallpaper paper has such a strong vertical pattern, it's perfect for cutting strips. Trim as shown and punch for a lacy look. Cut individual roses from the remaining paper and use as embellishments. Cut the flower mats, using the same technique as for the strips. Glue the photos to the mat center and detail with a pen.

Paper Pizazz™: rose wallpaper (*Romantic Papers*)
Solid Paper Pizazz™: pink (*Plain Pastels*)
Ruler: border edge Déjà Views by C-Thru® Ruler Co.
Teardrop and small circle punches: Family Treasures
Page designer: Debbie Peterson

Title Pages

Title pages can be used at least two ways. One is to be the first page in your scrapbook. This is particularly effective if the entire album focuses on a theme represented by the title page. Title pages can also be designed to create mini-sections within your memory books. Creating "chapters" in your scrapbook helps to organize the pages. They will have definite order—a beginning and an end, rather than looking like they were just put in anywhere. Title pages provide a smooth transition from birthday photos to everyday snapshots to Christmas photos. This technique is like many of the others in that, once you know it, you'll find lots of creative ways to use it.

You may want to have a chapter just for photos of a special trip, or to feature a special person or time in your life. The title page at the top of page 92 introduces pages of photos from 1998's Christmas celebration. The example at the top of page 93 shows the following photos are of their wedding day. We bet you can guess what the title pages on pages 90 and 91 introduce! Yep! Fabulous vacations with Mickey Mouse!

Other embellishments, like punches or stickers, can be used on your title page to support the theme of the photos to follow. The page at the bottom of page 89 leaves no doubt that fun pictures of Halloween celebrations are to come. The Punch-Out™ and die cut used on the title page at the bottom of page 92 suggest you'll see lots of photos of the wonderful things Gary and Beth did during their favorite season of the year!

Title pages provide a striking effect in your memory album, yet they're simple to create! This chapter shows you many examples that prove organizing your scrapbook has never been so easy!

This chapter's background paper is from *Paper Pizazz™ Light Great Backgrounds.*

A page like this might begin an album documenting the year of 1992 or the friendship of Katie and Adrienne. With the strong red in the photo, the page designer could have spelled the girls' names using only red letters (like the 1992), but adding the blue and gold letters allows the names to stand out! After arranging the journaling on three sides, use a border and coordinating corner Punch-Outs™ to fill the empty areas. The black and white dot background is a perfect setting for all the page elements.

Paper Pizazz™: black with white do (*Stripes, Checks & Dots*), burgundy tri dot (*Dots, Plaids, Checks & Stripes*)

Solid Paper Pizazz™: hunter green (*Solid Jewel Tones*)

Punch-Outs™: letters, numbers (*Pretty ABC*), cherry border, cherry cluster (*Pretty*)

Blue pen: Zig® Writer by EK Success Ltd.

Page designer: Sally Clarke

Older black and white photos may have a slight yellow tone, so design a scrapbook page that complements these colors. The gold letters used on this page could even be used throughout the album! The swirled background paper, with its many golds and yellows, picks up the colors of the photo and embellishments, allowing several shades of gold to coexist. The letters and numbers are matted in black to match the photo.

Paper Pizazz™: brown swirl (*For Black & White Photos*)

Solid Paper Pizazz™: black (*Solid Jewel Tones*)

Punch-Outs™: letters, numbers (*Pretty ABC*)

Cutouts: gold swirls (*Black & White Photos*)

Page designer: Sally Clarke

Here's a technique you can use for each year's school photo. Choose a patterned paper with two colors. Select plain papers in the same colors and cut 1" blocks. Mat each block in the opposite color, then place the sticker in the center of the block, alternating colors as shown. Add a cutout to the corner to summarize the year's achievements. The mortar board is perfect for the last year of high school, but a crayon would be better for 1st grade.

Paper Pizazz™: green checks (*Dots, Checks, Plaids & Stripes*)
Solid Paper Pizazz™: white (*Plain Pastels*), hunter green (*Solid Muted Tones*)
Cutout: mortarboard (*School Days*)
Alphabet stickers: Pebbles Inc.
Page designer: Shauna Wright for Paper Hearts

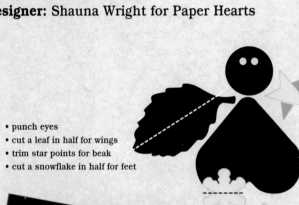

• punch eyes
• cut a leaf in half for wings
• trim star points for beak
• cut a snowflake in half for feet

If you want to make a page of a special event, but have only one photo, create a scene and use lettering to fill the remaining area. This is also a good idea when designing title pages, because you can fill in the detail of the day with other pages. A scenic paper starts this page, providing an instant background. Use patterned scissors on one side of each letter for a unique look. (Tree pattern on page 138.)

Paper Pizazz™: campfire (*Great Outdoors*)
Solid Paper Pizazz™: black, gray, brown (*Solid Jewel Tones*), white, pale orange (*Plain Pastels*)
½" wide star, ⅞" wide heart, 1/16" hole and ½" long teardrop punches: McGill, Inc.
½" wide circle punch: Marvy® Uchida
Leaf and snowflake punches: Family Treasures
Ghost stickers: Hambly Studios, Inc.
Decorative scissors: bat wings, deckle by Fiskars®, Inc.
Page designer: Debbie Peterson

Here's a striking way to use a page of repeating blocks. Glue a double-matted photo of Mickey Mouse to the page at an angle, then anchor the photo with his matted face glued to each corner. Un-matted faces of his friends are glued to each page corner. Arrange the titling along the upper and lower page; as this page begins the album, simply spell "Walt Disney World" rather than a more elaborate description of the trip. Use the journaling as a decorative border. If you need to say more, two lines of journaling could be added without changing the look of the page.

Paper Pizazz™: postage stamp faces (*Disney's Playtime with Mickey & Friends*)
Solid Paper Pizazz™: red (*Plain Brights*), black (*Solid Jewel Tones*), white (*Plain Pastels*)
Alphabet stickers: Pebbles in My Pocket
Page designer: Nancy Church for Pebbles in my Pocket

What a perfect combination—Mickey Mouse patterned paper with Mickey Mouse ABC's! Because the patterned paper has horizontal lines of images, it's easy to cut apart and use in strips as shown here. Then arrange one 4" and two 2" wide black circles into the classic mouse head and glue a slightly smaller photo in the center. Notice the placement of the mouse head allows room for each word.

Paper Pizazz™: Mickey silhouettes (*Disney's Playtime with Mickey & Friends*)
Solid Paper Pizazz™: goldenrod (*Plain Brights*), black (*Solid Jewel Tones*)
Punch-Outs™: letters & numbers (*Disney's Mickey & Friends ABC*)
Page designer: Shauna Wright for Paper Hearts

Don't you want to find out more about this party? These patterned papers are a perfect complement for each other—the more elaborate Disney hearts paper is a great background while the confetti hearts is better near the photo. Write simple letters on white paper, cut into squares and double-mat. Overlap them above and below the photo for a casual and fun look. Minnie celebrates the party, ending the page like an exclamation point.

Paper Pizazz™: Daisy, Minnie hearts (*Disney's Playtime with Mickey & Friends*), confetti hearts (*Birthday*)

Solid Paper Pizazz™: aqua, pink, purple (*Plain Brights*)

Cutout: Minnie (*Disney's Playtime with Mickey & Friends*)

Blue pen: Zig® Writer by EK Success Ltd.

Decorative scissors: canyon cutter, camelback by McGill, Inc.

Page designers: LeNae Gerig and Susan Cobb for Hot Off The Press

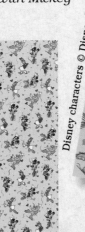

Disney characters © Disney Enterprises, Inc.

Disney characters © Disney Enterprises, Inc.

Disney characters © Disney Enterprises, Inc.

Make this page from the remainder of the paper used on page 90! Use the outer edges of the paper on this page, then cover the cut-up center with black. Journal and embellish at the same time with Mickey ABCs. The total effect is different from the page on 90, yet the individual elements are very similar!

Paper Pizazz™: postage stamp faces (*Disney's Playtime With Mickey & Friends*), black with dots (*Bright Great Backgrounds*)

Solid Paper Pizazz™: black (*Solid Jewel Tones*), red, goldenrod (*Plain Brights*)

Punch-Outs™: letters & numbers (*Disney's Mickey & Friends ABC*)

Decorative scissors: ripple by Fiskars® Inc.

White pen: Zig® Opaque Writer by EK Success Ltd.

Page designer: Katie Hacker for Hot Off The Press

Titling pages are meant to provide the basic information for the pages to come. They should have a large title, a photo depicting the main "characters" and perhaps the year; they are not supposed to contain every detail of the event. Use coordinating papers, Punch-Outs™ and stickers to connect your page elements. The white area surrounding the plaid "Christmas at our House" Punch-Out™ makes it stand out, but the green mat separates it from the ivy paper even more. The red tartan side strips match the plaid in the title. The sticker-decorated numbers complete the page.

Paper Pizazz™: ivy (*Floral Papers*), red tartan (*Christmas*)
Solid Paper Pizazz™: red, green (*Plain Brights*)
Punch-Outs™: "Christmas at our House" (*Titles*)
Red Design Line and holly leaf stickers: ©Mrs. Grossman's Paper Company
Die cuts: numbers by Ellison® Craft & Design
Decorative scissors: deckle by Family Treasures
Page designer: Katie Hacker for Hot Off The Press

The green strips are an easy-to-do decorative element (see pages 130–137 for more strip ideas). The mixture of natural-colored papers works together to accent the autumn theme used in the pages of this album.

Paper Pizazz™: brown plaid (*Our Vacations*), cedar handmade (*Handmade Papers*)
Solid Paper Pizazz™: orange, hunter green (*Solid Muted Colors*)
Punch-Outs™: "Autumn Fun" (*Titles*)
Maple leaf die cut: Ellison® Craft & Design
Page designer: LeNae Gerig for Hot Off The Press

Special photos can set the scene for a wedding album! The viewer is immediately drawn to the joined hands in this photo because the page elements lead to them. The large letters are easy to read, adding information without competing for attention. The gold paper separates the white patterned papers and picks up the brown and gold details. This page really gives a good idea of what the rest of the album will look like!

Paper Pizazz™: antique lace (*Our Wedding Day*), diagonal ribbons (*Romantic Papers*)

Solid Paper Pizazz™: metallic gold (*Metallic Papers*), green (*Solid Muted Tones*)

Punch-Outs™: letters (*Pretty ABC*)

Decorative scissors: Colonial by Fiskars®, Inc.

Photograph: Capell's Creations

Page designer: Katie Hacker for Hot Off The Press

For a trip to England, start the page with traditional touches such as the photos corners, pinstripes, calligraphy lettering and curlicues. The stickers around the edges of the page give it some exuberance, reflecting the excitement of traveling, but the remaining elements are ALL English.

Paper Pizazz™: burgundy pinstripe (*Stripes, Checks & Dots*)

Solid Paper Pizazz™: dark blue, white (*Plain Pastels*)

Photo corners: Fiskars®, Inc.

Stamp stickers: The Gifted Line®

White pen: Zig® Opaque Writer by EK Success Ltd.

Black pen: Calligraphy™ by Marvy® Uchida

Decorative scissors: deckle by Family Treasures

Page designer: LeNae Gerig for Hot Off The Press

The tropical butterflies & flowers were really amazing. You can just see a little blue on the brown one— it was too fast for me! I snapped this pic of Lou on the way out.

BUTTERFLIES!

"On the Road again...

OREGON

SPEED LIMIT ??

ROAD TRIP!

94

Span-A -Spread

While we usually work on our scrapbook pages one at a time, remember that when your album is open the pages will be viewed as one unit; that is, as a spread of two pages. Realizing this provides some very inspiring page designs! A good spread might look like one continuous album page. This chapter shows examples of how to create one large page using designs to span that spread.

Many of the examples in this chapter show how to use a single design element, usually a large pattern, to suggest a theme. The shape, like the nutcracker on page 96 or the whale on page 100, is cut in half and glued onto each album page so that when the pages are laid together the shape looks whole. Another technique is to use elements from a single Paper Pizazz™ sheet cut apart to create a design on two album pages as shown on page 99.

Spread elements join the pages and move the eye through both to introduce the theme of the photos in a very creative way. This type of album page design can provide just the Pizazz your album needs. And, with the examples shown in this chapter, you'll be spanning those spreads in no time!

Build this nutcracker, then cut him down the middle and glue one half to each page. The edges might not line up perfectly, but the image is distinctive enough to link the pages at first glance. *(Nutcracker pattern on page 139.)*

Paper Pizazz™: red & green dots, green plaid (*Ho Ho Ho!!!*)

Solid Paper Pizazz™: red, green, blue (*Plain Brights*), burgundy, black (*Solid Jewel Tones*), white, buff (*Plain Pastels*)

Alphabet stickers: Déjà Views by C-Thru® Ruler Co.

⅛", ¼", ⁷⁄₁₆" **wide circles, ⁵⁄₁₆" long teardrop, ¼" long oval, rectangle, spiral, and snowflake punches**: Family Treasures

Page designer: Anne-Marie Spencer for Hot Off The Press

Good spreads look like a continuous page. Notice the photos are placed in mirror-image locations. The hand drawn swirls and curlicues add a playful border on the barnwood paper. (Tree pattern on page 138.)

Paper Pizazz™: barnwood (*Country*), green checks (*Dots, Checks, Plaids & Stripes*), pine boughs (*Christmas*)

Solid Paper Pizazz™: metallic gold (*Metallic Papers*), white (*Plain Pastels*), red, yellow (*Plain Brights*)

⅛" **and** ¼" **wide punches**: Family Treasures

Bow punch: Marvy® Uchida

Tree die cut: Ellison® Craft & Design

Gold pen: DecoColor™ by Marvy® Uchida

Decorative scissors: deckle by Family Treasures

Page designer: Becky Goughnour for Hot Off The Press

96

Use a flag as a page background. The subtle patterns of these red, white and blue papers allow the flag to stand out, but are interesting enough to hold your attention. Then mat the photos so they match.

Paper Pizazz™: blue stars (*Adult Birthdays*), burgundy tri-dot, burgundy pinstripe, navy checks, navy tri-dot (*Dots, Checks, Plaids & Stripes*)

Solid Paper Pizazz™: red, blue (*Solid Jewel Tones*), white (*Plain Pastels*)

Star punch: Marvy® Uchida

Page designer: Terri Carter for Paper Hearts

Making a paper flag background of the country you've visited is a great idea! And it's even better if the flag goes on a spread. Mat a flag on contrasting papers, to add more colors to a bi-colored theme. Mat the photos on assorted plain papers found in the background papers. (Canada's maple leaf pattern on page 141.)

Paper Pizazz™: blue chalky (*Bright Great Backgrounds*), red & blue plaid (*Masculine Papers*)

Solid Paper Pizazz™: pale purple, purple, deep blue, hunter green, orange, yellow (*Solid Muted Colors*), red (*Plain Brights*), white (*Plain Pastels*)

Decorative scissors: deckle by Family Treasures

Page designer: Katie Hacker for Hot Off The Press

97

It's easy to make a pond scene, complete with lily pads and frogs, using punches and a little creativity. Draw a wavy pond (no pattern needed) on patterned paper and glue to plain paper. Cut the photos into lily pads, mat and glue on the pond. Make markers and signs to hold the journaling. (Sign patterns on page 139; lily pad pattern on page 142; frog punch pattern on page 34.)

Paper Pizazz™: magic stones, purple chalky (*Bright Great Backgrounds*), barn-wood (*Country*)

Solid Paper Pizazz™: green (*Plain Brights*), white, buff (*Plain Pastels*), black (*Solid Jewel Tones*)

¼", ½", 1¼" wide circles, ½", 1¼" wide hearts, tulip, and sun punches: McGill, Inc.

Decorative scissors: deckle by Family Treasures

Page designer: Debbie Peterson

Enlarge the outline of any state and cut from road map paper (that way you know the paper is acid-free). Mat and place on a background paper appropriate to the state. Write the destination in large letters, mat and glue where it can introduce the page. Stickers expand on the road trip theme. (Arrow pattern on page 140.)

Paper Pizazz™: trees, road map (*Our Vacations*)

Solid Paper Pizazz™: hunter green, olive, burgundy, orange, brown, deep blue (*Solid Muted Colors*), black (*Solid Jewel Tones*)

Road signs, glasses and message stickers: Frances Meyer, Inc.®

Green pen: Zig® Writer by EK Success Ltd.

Decorative scissors: deckle by Family Treasures

Page designer: Katie Hacker for Hot Off The Press

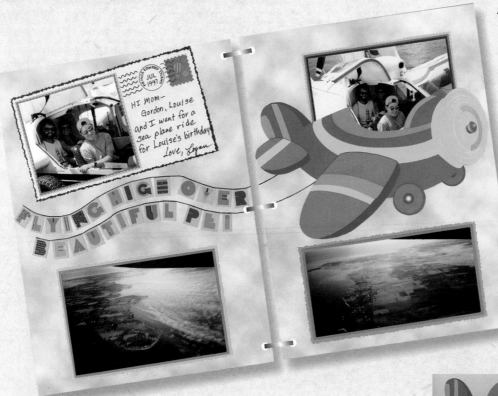

The spreads on this page demonstrate the different ways you can use Quick & Easy papers by cutting them apart. This spread uses one airplane and fills the remaining area with matted photos and clever journaling.

Paper Pizazz™: clouds (*Vacation*), two airplanes (*Quick & Easy*)

Solid Paper Pizazz™: goldenrod, orange, blue, red (*Plain Brights*), white (*Plain Pastels*), black (*Solid Jewel Tones*)

Alphabet stickers: ©Mrs. Grossman's Paper Company

Decorative scissors: deckle and small scallop by Family Treasures

Page designer: Sally Clarke

This page uses all the elements of the Quick & Easy airplane paper, including the Earth. Photos of Ari and her mother are cropped into window shapes and placed directly on the planes, turning them into elaborate mats. Stickers and journaling fill the remaining areas.

Paper Pizazz™: clouds (*Vacation*), two airplanes (*Quick & Easy*)

Solid Paper Pizazz™: yellow, orange, blue (*Plain Brights*)

Punch-Outs™: suit cases (*Vacation*)

Border Lines: ©Mrs. Grossman's Paper Company

Confetti stickers: ©Mrs. Grossman's Paper Company

Blue and dark blue pens: Zig® Writer by EK Success Ltd.

Decorative scissors: cloud, scallop by Fiskars®, Inc.

Page designer: Katie Hacker for Hot Off The Press

The orca is first glued together, then cut in half for each page. It jumps out of a matted blue ripple paper. The navy checks background paper works well with the stark pattern of the orca while accenting the blues of the ripple paper. The remaining matting papers add color to the page and move the eye from photo to photo. (Orca pattern on page 141.)

Paper Pizazz™: navy checks (*Dots, Checks, Plaids & Stripes*), blue ripple, bright gathers (*Bright Great Backgrounds*)
Solid Paper Pizazz™: lime, blue, green, pink (*Plain Brights*), white (*Plain Pastels*), black (*Solid Jewel Tones*)
Alphabet die cuts: Accu/Cut® Systems
Page designer: Becky Goughnour for Hot Off The Press

Sky, clouds or grass paper are often chosen as backgrounds because they go with anything. The fern paper is a natural backdrop for flowers. Cut the purple daisies paper into a butterfly, then mat the photos and journaling on bright plain papers. (Butterfly pattern on page 141.)

Paper Pizazz™: bright ferns, purple daisies (*Floral Papers*)
Solid Paper Pizazz™: orange, light orange, purple, lime, green, blue, red, light blue, yellow (*Plain Brights*)
Alphabet die cut: Accu/Cut® Systems
Decorative scissors: ripply by McGill, Inc.
Page designer: Katie Hacker for Hot Off The Press

Die cuts can be cut quickly so you can use lots of them! Arrange the balloons like a bouquet, then use a pen to draw their tails. Glue the matted photos in the empty areas and add a few escaped balloons in the remaining areas.

Paper Pizazz™:
   lavender hearts & lines (*Light Great Backgrounds*)
Solid Paper Pizazz™:
   red, green, blue, pink, goldenrod (*Plain Brights*), deep purple (*Solid Muted Colors*)
Balloon and heart die cuts: Ellison® Craft & Design
Decorative scissors: corkscrew by Fiskars®, Inc.
Page designer: LeNae Gerig for Hot Off The Press

A tree against the hazy sky forms the backdrop for these trick-or-treaters. Place black and brown ink on a small makeup sponge, then dab on the clouds paper to make fog. Silhouette cropping the individual children gives the page a fun look—like they were coming to your door! (Tree pattern on page 140.)

Paper Pizazz™: clouds (*Vacation*), crushed suede (*Black & White Photos*)
Solid Paper Pizazz™: goldenrod (*Plain Brights*)
Punch-Outs™: pumpkins, bat, cat, spider (*Holidays & Seasons*)

Tree die cut: Accu/Cut® Systems
Black and brown stamp ink: Stampendous!®
Page designer: LeNae Gerig for Hot Off The Press

Here is a background that doesn't match anything! Yet, it goes perfectly with the photos proving theme can be as important as color when choosing papers. Bright mats and patterns flesh out the disco theme. Paisley paper mats the title. (Lava lamp pattern on page 138.)

Paper Pizazz™: daisies, blue paisley (*50's & 60's Papers*)

Solid Paper Pizazz™: pink, yellow, orange, blue, green, purple (*Plain Brights*), black (*Solid Jewel Tones*), white (*Plain Pastels*)

Alphabet die cuts: Accu/Cut® Systems

Decorative scissors: cloud, scallop by Fiskars®, Inc.

Page designer: Katie Hacker for Hot Off The Press

Patterned strips border the page edges, then mat the photos with patterned papers using the same colors. The watermelon spans the spread and hand-drawn ants march across the pages, helping the movement. Notice the photos are first matted on plain paper followed by striped or plaid paper mats. (Watermelon pattern on page 140.)

Paper Pizazz™: Christmas plaid, red & white stripes, green plaid (*Ho Ho Ho!!!*)

Solid Paper Pizazz™: green, light green, red (*Plain Brights*), hunter green, black (*Solid Jewel Tones*), white (*Plain Pastels*)

Decorative scissors: deckle by Fiskars®, Inc.

Page designer: Amberly Beck

Arrange dozens of 1" wide squares into a block quilt on plain purple paper. Mat on white, then use a scalloped ruler to cut a border. Outline the border with a colored pen. Add baby stickers around the edge, then glue the photos to the quilt—no matting is needed!

Paper Pizazz™: pastel dots, pastel quilt, pastel hearts (*Baby*)

Solid Paper Pizazz™: pink, purple, white (*Plain Pastels*)

Baby theme stickers: ©Mrs. Grossman's Paper Company

Scallop-edged ruler: Westrim® Crafts

Purple pens: Zig® Writer by EK Success Ltd.

Decorative scissors: scallop by Fiskars®, Inc.

Page designer: Amberly Beck

Sky and grass go together like a summer day. Once this scene is made, add a train. It's cute, bright, festive and provides a great spot for journaling. It's made with a technique called Scrapliqué (see pages 116-118). Mix and match any papers with bright colors! (Train pattern on page 142.)

Paper Pizazz™: clouds (*Our Vacations*), happy birthday, colorful stripes, lines & dots (*Birthday*), blue stars (*Adult Birthday*), grass (*Pets*), barnwood (*Country*)

Solid Paper Pizazz™: red, goldenrod, orange (*Plain Brights*), black (*Solid Jewel Tones*)

Scissors: ripple by Fiskars® Inc.

Train pattern: Kathy Christenson

Page Designer: Katie Hacker for Hot Off The Press

Clever Cuts

We've discovered three new ways to cut a page and create a three to six page photo journal. We've also found an exciting new approach to making patterns for your pages. With all the smart uses we've found for your scissors, you'll soon see why we've called this chapter Clever Cuts!

The Center Cuts technique was created by Katie Hacker who works at Hot Off The Press. We're so proud of her! It's a new technique used to create a six-page photo-story. This is a terrific method that offers a way to include many photos of the same event to tell your tale! It's really quite simple. We've included step-by-step photos and full instructions for creating Center Cuts on page 106. Plus, you'll find tips in the section on how you can adapt this technique to best tell your story.

Cutting Edge is a technique that creates a three-page spread! The spread is fun to design and leaves plenty of room for extra photos. Pages 110 and 111 offer some great ways to help you do this for your own album.

We just heard about Peek-a-Boo Pages on the internet. They're another way to link many album pages to a single theme. The instructions and examples of this technique start on page 112. Each one shows you just how to complete this wonderful effect!

Our final technique for cutting things another way comes on page 116. It's a method we call Scrapliqué. We've also heard it referred to as paper piecing. Wonderful theme related shapes are pieced together from scraps of patterned papers and glued to your pages. Make a kitty with a sweet bow (page 116), a Halloween scarecrow (page 117), or more!

So, this chapter offers you four new methods for using your scissors in truly inventive ways. The effects will shine through in your wonderful scrapbook pages!

This chapter's background paper is *Paper Pizazz*™ pink tiles sold only by the sheet.

Center Cuts

A new twist on a two page spread—moveable center pages that show a different page with each turn.

The uncovered elements, such as the titling and outer photos on these pages, are as important as the moveable center pages. If you have different journaling on each center page, it will make the viewer look at the outer photos differently each time. It makes the whole collection of pages a complete story. (Heart pattern on page 141.)

Paper Pizazz™: bright ferns, white rose buds, delphinium (*Floral Papers*)

Solid Paper Pizazz™: metallic gold (*Metallic Papers*), hunter green, pale purple, dark blue, pale green (*Solid Muted Colors*)

Punch-Outs™: letters & numbers (*Pretty ABC*)

Decorative scissors: deckle, wave by Family Treasures

Page designer: Katie Hacker for Hot Off The Press

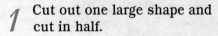

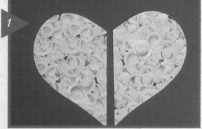

1 Cut out one large shape and cut in half.

2 Glue one half on each side of a two-page spread.

3 Glue two paper sheets back to back, then cut out another large shape and cut in half. Repeat as desired.

4 Finish your inner pages, then run a thin line of glue along the inside edge of each shape and place inside sheet protectors. This will hold it in place. If you are using an album with permanent pages, glue one side of each shape directly onto the album page and cut around it.

Center-cut pages work really well with events that have different stages, people or themes running through the event. Each time you turn a page, a different part is shown.

Arrange the photos and journaling on the first and last pages so the half ball covers them as you turn the pages. (Ball pattern on page 141.)

Tip: With a slightly different center shape, other paper combinations include: soccer with grass paper—gold balls with grass paper—or footballs with field paper.

Paper Pizazz™: basketball court, basketballs (*Sports*)
Solid Paper Pizazz™: blue, red, yellow (*Plain Brights*), white (*Plain Pastels*)
Punch-Outs™: basketballs (*Kids*), banner (*School*)
Decorative scissors: bat wings by Fiskars®, Inc.
Page designer: Katie Hacker for Hot Off The Press

Football field (*Sports*)

Footballs (*Sports*)

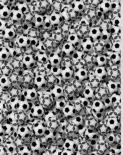

Soccer balls (*Sports*)

Grass (*Pets*)

When arranging photos, don't let a turning page cover half of someone's face! A small amount of overlap looks nice, but either cover the photo completely or let it stand out. The photos on page 107 are arranged so new photos show with each turn of the page; however, only the photos on the star change on this page. Each set of pages on 107 told about a different part of the basketball season, whereas these pages tell one complete story. (Star pattern on page 138.)

Paper Pizazz™: holly (*Ho Ho Ho!!!*), burgundy with white stars, burgundy pinstripe (*Dots, Checks, Plaids & Stripes*)

Solid Paper Pizazz™: metallic gold (*Metallic Papers*), green, red (*Plain Brights*)

Punch-Outs™: "Merry Christmas" (*Titles*)

¼" wide circle and holly leaf punches: Family Treasures

Decorative scissors: deckle by Fiskars®, Inc.

Page designer: Katie Hacker for Hot Off The Press

Tip: Any of these papers will work with the center-cut star to create pages with a different theme— baby, fun or celebration.

sun & moon (*Childhood*)

hearts, coils & stars (*Childhood*) fireworks (*Adult Birthday*)

The previous pages have featured general shapes that could be used on many occasions; however, almost any symmetrical object can be used to form a center-cut spread. A hot-air balloon that changes color each time you turn the page sets the tone for this series. You could use a car from a car show, a teddy bear or rattle for a baby page, a fish for a fishing trip, or even a flower from your garden. The possibilities are endless. Find a patterned paper in your theme, then borrow a shape and give it a try! (Balloon pattern on page 141.)

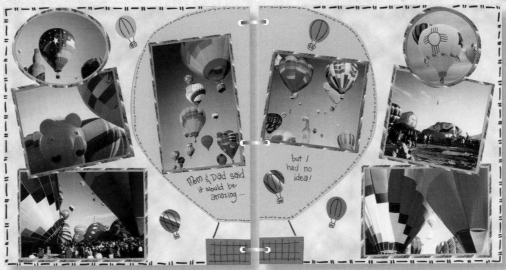

Paper Pizazz™: clouds (*Our Vacations*), colorful stripes (*Great Backgrounds*)

Solid Paper Pizazz™: green, purple, orange, goldenrod, blue, aqua, red, yellow (*Plain Brights*)

Balloon punch: Family Treasures

Decorative scissors: deckle by Family Treasures

Page designer: Katie Hacker for Hot Off The Press

Cutting Edge

Our solution for linking three pages into one story—use a shape on the right edge of the last page and cut the edges of the first and second pages so you can see the shape on every page.

Because the fir tree links the pages, it isn't necessary to use exactly the same papers. In this series, three very different papers show different stages of the trip. This is a nice trick to have, because many trips—a family vacation for example—have several different destinations before they are through. Using this technique, you can use a themed paper for each destination as long as you have one element on the cutting edge that remains the same. (Tree pattern on page 138.)

Paper Pizazz™: moose & deer, outdoor adventure, sunset (*Great Outdoors*)
Solid Paper Pizazz™: hunter green, oatmeal, blue, dark blue, pale green, burgundy (*Solid Muted Colors*)
Christmas tree die cut: Accu/Cut® Systems
Green pen: Marvy® Uchida
Decorative scissors: ripple by Fiskars®, Inc.
Page designer: Katie Hacker for Hot Off The Press

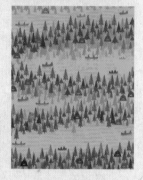

Thank goodness the weather cleared up the second day! We had a beautiful hike in the mountains.
September 1998

Extra large die cuts are perfect for making this kind of page. Select a large die cut, such as the oak leaf used on this page, and glue it to the back page as shown. Place the remaining pages back to back and use the die to cut the edges so the leaf shows through!

The first page establishes color and theme. The autumn leaves paper, used as the background on the first page, forms the matting and border stripes on the second and third pages. In contrast, the plain backgrounds on the middle pages provide the matting on the first page. Use inversion like this whenever possible—it's simple and very effective! (Large oak leaf pattern on page 142.)

Tip: The image in the upper left corner of the first page is a color photocopy of an actual poem as written by the child. It's great to include these kind of items on your pages.

Paper Pizazz™: autumn leaves (*Our Holidays & Seasons*)
Solid Paper Pizazz™: hunter green, orange (*Solid Jewel Tones*), light orange, pale yellow, brown (*Solid Muted Colors*)
Cardstock: 12"x12" brown, 12"x12" orange
Oak leaf punch: Family Treasures
Maple leaf punch: McGill, Inc.
Oak leaf die cuts: Accu/Cut® Systems
Decorative scissors: ripply by McGill, Inc.
Page designer: LeNae Gerig for Hot Off The Press

BIRTHDAY BOY

ZAKKERY's 4th Birthday Party

Peek-A-Boo Pages

In a series of three (or four...or five) pages, cut a shape in the first pages to see something on the last page. Here, a balloon die cut is glued to the last page with a balloon-shaped hole in pages 1 and 2. When page 1 is closed, you can see the journaling about Zakkery's 4th birthday party.

Paper Pizazz™: black with dots, stripes on black (*Bright Great Backgrounds*)

Solid Paper Pizazz™: red, goldenrod, blue, green (*Plain Brights*)

Punch-Outs™: "Birthday boy," "Just What I Wanted" (*Titles*)

¾" and ½" wide circle punches: McGill, Inc.

Balloon die cut: Accu/Cut® Systems

Decorative scissors: ripply by McGill, Inc.

Red pen: Zig® Writer by EK Success Ltd.

Page designer: LeNae Gerig for Hot Off The Press

~Pinata~

smile

Just What I Wanted!

ZAKKERY's 4th Birthday Party

On a four-page spread, the hole will be in pages 2 and 3; however, it needs to work with every turn of the page!

In this series, the square holding the stork is the same size as the opposite square showing Mason in his hat. When the page is turned (as shown below) the empty square shows the stork but now we see Mason has company!

To give variety in most Paper Pizazz™ books, usually there's only one paper of a certain design, such as the baby items paper from Paper Pizazz™ Baby. However, many of these same papers are also sold by the sheet so you can get many copies of a particular design to make pages like these.

My mom and dad say sometimes I get a look in my eyes that makes me seem like I know something they don't know.

My name is Mason. I'm 6 months old.

Mom and I have a good time. She stays home with me all day — we sing a lot.

This is my friend Emma. She's 10 days younger than me.

Our moms have been friends for a long time, so we've known each other since before we were even born! We like to listen to music and we talk to each other. We have a secret language that grownups don't understand. Even when I get tired and cranky, Emma sticks by my side.

Paper Pizazz™: baby items (*Baby*), pink & blue plaid (*Light Great Backgrounds*)

Solid Paper Pizazz™: blue, pink, mint, light blue, yellow (*Plain Pastels*)

Punch-Outs™: sun, lamb, stork, pacifier (*Baby*)

Decorative scissors: deckle by Family Treasures

Page designer: Katie Hacker for Hot Off The Press

The many photos, embellishments and journaling as well as the constantly shifting layout gives the viewer a lot to explore on this wonderful series of pages! Notice how each individual element reveals a different character complementing the series as a whole.

Unlike the previous pages, which carry one peak-a-boo shape through all the pages, this page starts with a small shape that gradually gets bigger, providing a different crop with each view. The original octagon "expands" into an old-fashioned rectangle on the third page. This allows an easy way to introduce the next woman and relationship in the story. On the same page, an oval is added allowing another element (and character) from the fifth page to show through.

Papers are also an important part of the connection between these pages. Using plain burgundy paper with a gold pen on the second page and the burgundy tri-dot on the third page connects papers on the the first patterned page to the rest of the series. Then the burgundy paper shows through to the brown crushed suede background of the last pages providing a neat connection between the first and last elements.

Paper Pizazz™: tapestry (*Pretty Papers*), burgundy tri-dot (*Dots, Checks, Plaids & Stripes*), crushed suede, letters (*Black & White Photos*), cork board (*School Days*)

Solid Paper Pizazz™: metallic gold, metallic copper (*Metallic Papers*), brown, buff, brick, ivory (*Solid Muted Tones*), black (*Solid Jewel Tones*)

Cutouts: gold embellishments, gold frames (*Embellishments*), silver frames (*Black & White Photos*)

Corner punch: Family Treasures

Decorative scissors: deckle by Fiskars®, Inc.

Gold pen: Gel Writer by Marvy® Uchida

Page designer: Sally Clarke

In this series, the Peek-A-Boo hole is in page 2 and 3. The oval shows one view of the cathedral, but when the page is turned, you see this photo is really a rectangle! The same hole shows the child photo without a green marble mat.

Paper Pizazz™: oatmeal handmade (*Handmade Papers*), green marble (*Very Pretty Papers*)
Solid Paper Pizazz™: white, ivory, pale yellow (*Solid Pastel Papers*), hunter green, gray (*Solid Muted Tones*)
Music note punch: McGill, Inc.
Decorative scissors: deckle by Family Treasures
Green, blue, orange pens: Zig® Writers by EK Success Ltd.
Page designer: Stephanie Taylor

Scrapliqué

Scrapliqué, also known as paper piecing or paper quilting, combines patterns and different papers into one interesting object. It's really fabric appliqué using paper! Use two-way glue (which temporarily adheres the pattern pieces to a background paper) to hold the pieces in place until you are satisfied with the result. Then cut the background paper around the pieces for a thin mat and place on the page.

Accent your black and white cat with a scrapliqué kitty made of black and white paper patterns. These work from a single book of papers, ensuring the papers will work well together, but still be interesting enough to show off the technique (and your work). Use a white pen to draw the cat's features. Notice the background paper is used again for the kitty's bow. (Kitty pattern on page 121.)

Paper Pizazz™: purple chalky (*Bright Great Backgrounds*), black & white swirl, white dot on black, black checks, black & white handmade (*For Black & White Photos*)
Solid Paper Pizazz™: pale purple, blue (*Solid Muted Colors*), black (*Solid Jewel Tones*)
Decorative scissors: mini pinking by Fiskars®, Inc.
Kitty pattern: Kathy Christenson
Page designer: Katie Hacker for Hot Off The Press

The rounded photos work like drops that the whale has spouted to create a miniature scene. Each patterned paper uses teal and bright blue, but the effect is far from monotonous! Black mats separates each paper from the others, making each paper and photo pop off the page! (Whale pattern on page 121.)

Paper Pizazz™: tie dye, purple chalky, magic stones, green swizzle, blue tiles (*Bright Great Backgrounds*)
Solid Paper Pizazz™: black (*Solid Jewel Tones*)
Decorative scissors: deckle by Family Treasures
Whale pattern: Kathy Christenson
Page designer: Katie Hacker for Hot Off The Press

Each patterned paper in the buggy shares a set of pastel colors, but making use of the individual patterns makes each distinct from the next. The striped paper work well on the long areas, while the dotted papers are a nice contrast in the rounded portions. (Buggy pattern on page 119; bear pattern on page 120.)

Paper Pizazz™: blue tri dot (*Baby's First Year*), pastel stripes, pastel dots, pastel hearts (*Baby*)
Solid Paper Pizazz™: pink, yellow (*Plain Pastels*)
Alphabet stickers: Déjà Views by C-Thru® Ruler Co.
Decorative scissors: scallop, mini scallop by Fiskars®, Inc.
Buggy and bear patterns: Teresa Nelson
Page designer: Anne-Marie Spencer for Hot Off The Press

The burlap paper looks great as the scarecrow's pants because it's a texture that might actually be used for a real scarecrow. The barnwood paper for the fence works in a similar way. (Scarecrow and jack-o-lantern patterns on page 120.)

Paper Pizazz™: blue stars (*Adult Birthday*), candy corn (*Holidays & Seasons*), burlap, barnwood (*Country*), aqua embossed (*Bright Great Backgrounds*)
Solid Paper Pizazz™: black, brown (*Solid Jewel Tones*), tan (*Plain Pastels*), orange (*Plain Brights*)
Scissors: heartstrings by Fiskars®, Inc.
Scarecrow and jack-o-lantern patterns: Teresa Nelson
Page designer: Anne-Marie Spencer for Hot Off The Press

Scrapliqué pages are particularly good when you don't have a lot of photos of a particular subject or occasion, but really want to create a page of it. By choosing just the right object, you can instantly create a theme. The Western boot immediately sets up a horses theme, filling in the missing details of the photo. (Boot pattern on page 119.)

Paper Pizazz™: barnwood, denim (*Country*)
Solid Paper Pizazz™: red, green, orange (*Plain Brights*), dark brown, brown (*Solid Muted Colors*)
Brown and gold pens: Marvy® Uchida
Page designer: Melodie Jones

Each piece of this page has been chosen with great care to make a more realistic image: the clouds paper for the background, the grass for ground, bricks for the chimney and laser lace for the curtains. (House pattern on page 120.)

Paper Pizazz™: clouds (*Vacation*), gray & pink swirl (*Black & White Photos*), bricks (*Masculine Papers*), grass (*Pets*), laser lace (*Romantic Papers*)
Solid Paper Pizazz™: gray, yellow, burgundy (*Solid Muted Colors*), black (*Solid Jewel Tones*)
Alphabet stickers: Déjà Views™ by C-Thru®
Flower stickers: ©Mrs. Grossman's Paper Company
Decorative scissors: heartbeat by Fiskars®, Inc.
House pattern: Teresa Nelson
Page designer: Anne-Marie Spencer for Hot Off The Press

Brightly colored papers contrast with the bricks for realistic looking packages. (Kitty and stocking pattern on page 119.)

Paper Pizazz™: white dot on green (*Christmas*), red & green dots, white dot on red, red & white stripes, red tartan (*Ho Ho Ho!!!*) bricks (*Masculine Papers*)
Solid Paper Pizazz™: hunter green, black (*Solid Jewel Tones*), white, tan, pink (*Plain Pastels*)
Decorative scissors: provincial by Fiskars®, Inc.
White pen: Zig® Opaque Writer by EK Success Ltd.
Kitty and stocking pattern: Teresa Nelson
Page designer: Anne-Marie Spencer for Hot Off The Press

This page makes use of almost every technique—punches, matting, strips, drawn embellishments, and titling! The white punches glued to Santa's beard are great details! (Santa pattern on page 121.)

Paper Pizazz™: Christmas plaid, white dot on red (*Ho Ho Ho!!!*)
Solid Paper Pizazz™: red, green (*Plain Brights*), tan, pink, white (*Plain Pastels*), black (*Solid Jewel Tones*)
Punch-Outs™: "Merry Christmas" (*Christmas*)
Snowflake punch: Family Treasures
¼", ½" and 1¼" wide hole punches: McGill, Inc.
Corrugator: Fiskars®, Inc.
Decorative scissors: pinking by Fiskars®, Inc.
Green pen: Zig™ Writer by EK Success Ltd.
Page designer: Katie Hacker for Hot Off The Press

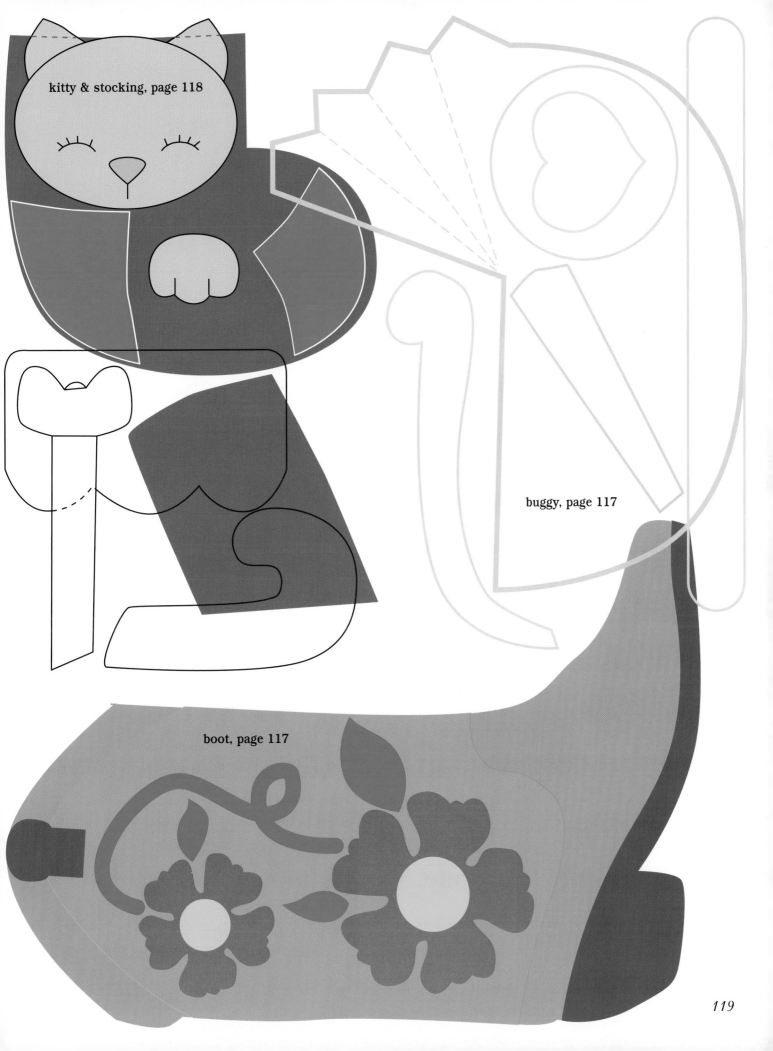

kitty & stocking, page 118

buggy, page 117

boot, page 117

teddy bear, page 117

jack-o'-lantern & scarecrow, page 117

house, page 118

120

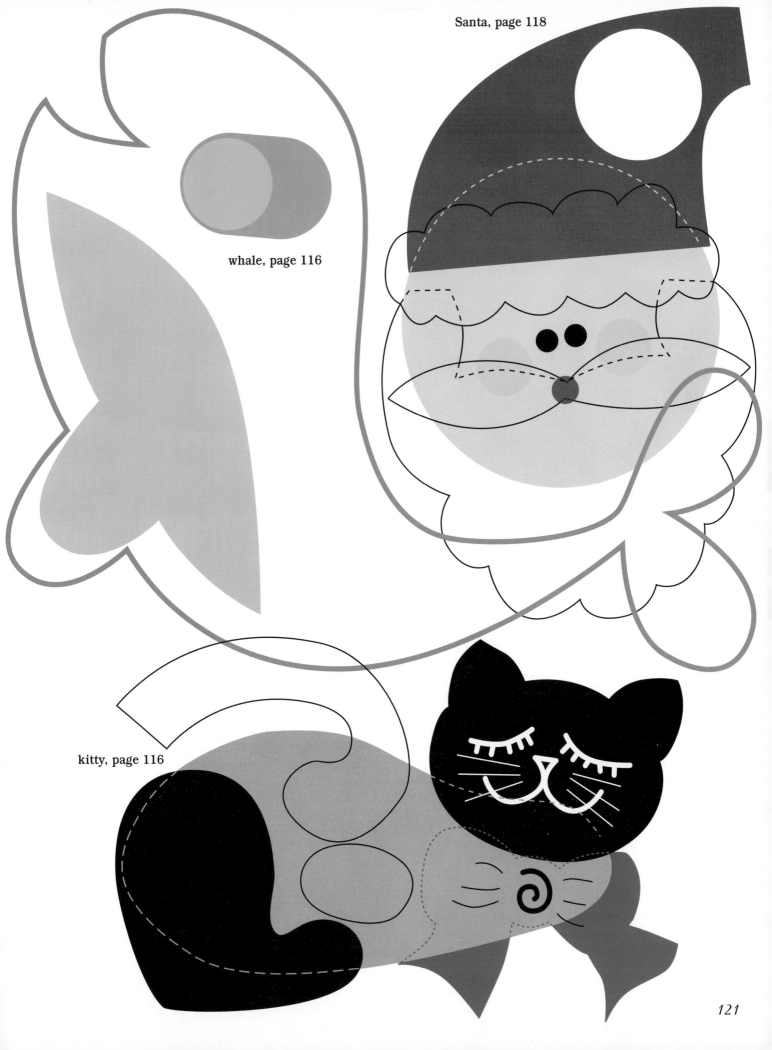

Santa, page 118

whale, page 116

kitty, page 116

October 1998

Ever since we first met, Becky and I have been the best of friends. We even share the same birthday!

2 WAY GLUE

ZIG

Cut Outs

Mr. Fultano's
FAMILY
PIZZA PARLOUR

Open Daily !

EVENING
DELIVERY

Pizza Night!
The gang got together for a little fun & games
Fall 1998

...at are litte boys made of ?

...yton and Alex   Spring '98.

Special Techniques

Throughout this book you've seen techniques to make exciting scrapbook pages. In this chapter we have a few final ideas to share with you.

Torn paper edges offer depth and texture to your pages. It's easy to do and a great look on the right page. Paper can be torn into vague or exact shapes. The torn mountains at the top of page 125 are perfect for the page design yet the simple appearance keeps the page feeling casual. The pine trees at the bottom of page 125 offer a dramatic border for this lighthearted portrait.

Pocket pages are a fun way to incorporate mementos into your album page designs. At the bottom of page 126 you'll see an idea for tucking tour pamphlets behind a journaled pocket! There are two great suggestions for saving wedding keepsakes with your album pages on page 127. Whether you want to display a child's artwork or a special greeting card, these examples will offer ideas!

Paper strips are an interesting way to define an album page design. Page 130 shows before and after views of two examples. Without the strip borders the pages lack focus—the eye doesn't know where to begin or end! What a difference a few strips of paper can make! Paper strips offer some great opportunities to have extra fun with your design, too. Draw dots on them like on page 133. Weave them as shown on page 135, or add punches to them as on page 132. You could even corrugate them like those on page 134!

Now that you know all about making scrapbook pages, we hope you'll share with your friends! Or with your co-workers. But most of all use this information to make wonderful scrapbook pages to share with family for years and years to come!

This chapter's background paper is from *Paper Pizazz™ Dots, Checks, Plaids & Stripes.*

Torn Paper—*an easy-to-do technique*

Use the blue stars paper as a night sky, then tear black strips of paper and place them behind the matted photos. Whether you see these as bat wings, clouds or simply shapes that direct the eye to the next object is up to you. Whatever you see, the technique works nicely to make a simple, attractive and atmospheric Halloween page.

Paper Pizazz™: blue stars (*Adult Birthday*)
Solid Paper Pizazz™: black (*Solid Jewel Tones*), white (*Plain Pastels*)
Punch-Outs™: ghosts, spider (*Holidays & Seasons*)
Decorative scissors: deckle by Family Treasures
Page designer: Debbie Peterson

© & ™ Ellison® Craft & Design

Torn strips work nicely to create realistic backgrounds. This page uses torn strips of brown paper in a variety of shades to make soil. Flowers emerge, each containing a photo; this is a nice way to use large die cuts or patterns. The background paper inspires a cloud for journaling. Stickers and drawn lines form the final details.

Paper Pizazz™: clouds (*Vacation*)
Solid Paper Pizazz™: yellow, red, green, pink, purple (*Plain Brights*), tan, light brown (*Solid Muted Colors*), white (*Plain Pastels*)
Insect stickers: ©Mrs. Grossman's Paper Co.
Sunflower die cut: Ellison® Craft & Design
Page designer: Ann Smith for Memory Lane

Large brown strips form mountains for a fuller page. The lightest paper is used in front with the darkest paper in the back to simulate depth. Cleverly, the destination spans the sky with the sun and the letter "O" sharing space.

Solid Paper Pizazz™: aqua, light blue (*Plain Brights*) buff, rust, brown, light brown (*Solid Muted Colors*)

Letter and sun die cuts: Ellison® Craft & Design

Page designer: Jane Blakesley

© & ™ Ellison® Craft & Design

Tearing shapes can provide a realistically irregular edge. These trees look more natural because their edges are not perfect! Mat the photo on red, then glue to the page top. Glue the trees across the lower page, then overlap with journaling. (Paper thickness will determine whether your torn pieces have a broad edge, as on this page, or a thinner edge.)

Solid Paper Pizazz™: red, hunter green (*Solid Jewel Tones*) white (*Plain Pastels*)

Letter stencil: Pebbles Inc.

Red pen: Graphic by Marvy® Uchida

Metallic red pen: Gel Roller by Marvy® Uchida

¼" wide circle punch: Family Treasures

Page designer: Heather Hummel

Pockets

The idea is simple—add a large shape to the page, glue it on three sides and insert treasures. It's a great way to include three-dimensional items related to the trip or experience, but that can't be easily placed on the page. This page uses papers creatively; the pizza slice is cut from the junk food paper to form a pocket and the Christmas plaid paper works as an Italian tablecloth.

Paper Pizazz™: junk food (*Teen*), Christmas plaid (*bulk papers*)
Solid Paper Pizazz™: green, light green (*Plain Brights*) brown, black (*Solid Jewel Tones*), white (*Plain Pastels*)
Decorative scissors: alligator by Fiskars®
Page designer: Katie Hacker for Hot Off The Press

The oval on this page has a dual purpose—it serves as the title area and a pocket. Because the viewer can remove the brochures and read about the places in the photos, the brochures form the journaling. The greens of the background paper work with the yellow and green of the matting papers; neither is one color, but many shades.

Paper Pizazz™: forest (*Our Vacations*), cedar handmade, green handmade (*Handmade Papers*)
Solid Paper Pizazz™: hunter green (*Solid Jewel Tones*)
Decorative scissors: alligator by Fiskars®, Inc.
Photo corners: Fiskars®, Inc.
Gold pen: DecoColor™ by Marvy® Uchida
Page designer: Katie Hacker for Hot Off The Press

Pockets can store a small piece of information, or they can be the focus of an entire page. This handkerchief, a wedding souvenir, is an important object on this page; however, it needs a sturdier pocket than the ones used on the last pages. Trim the pink lace paper around the edges, then cut a 7" long slit in the center. Glue the edges to the white paper, then place the handkerchief, photo and wedding invitation inside the opening as shown.

Paper Pizazz™: pink lace (*Pretty Papers*)
Solid Paper Pizazz™: white (*Plain Pastels*)
Decorative scissors: deckle by Fiskars®, Inc.
Gold and maroon pens: Zig® Writer by EK Success Ltd.
Page designer: Carol Dace

Larger pages are ideal for wedding albums because of the large number of keepsakes and photos to work with. This page allows room for a matted photo, titling and a large pocket for several keepsakes which might have otherwise taken up two pages.

Paper Pizazz™: roses, pink moiré (*Our Wedding*) laser lace (*Romantic Papers*)
Solid Paper Pizazz™: pink (*Plain Pastels*), white (*Solid Pastel Papers*)
Punch-Outs™: "Our Wedding Day" (*Titles*)
Decorative scissors: mini Victorian, Victorian by Family Treasures
Ribbon: 6" of ¼" wide pink satin
Page designer: LeNae Gerig for Hot Off The Press

laser lace

127

© & ™ Accu/Cut® Systems

Though you can copy and reduce a child's paintings to display them, sometimes it just isn't the same. Make one page to tell the story, then create a coordinating page (see pages 94–103 for tips) with a pocket to hold the art. The paper left over from the 12"x12" sheet of alphabet letters is used to create the top of the pocket.

Paper Pizazz™: alphabet letters (*Our School Days*)
Solid Paper Pizazz™: goldenrod, blue (*Plain Brights*)
Cutouts: crayon pack, crayons, paintbrush, splat, bus (*School Days*)
Star die cut: Accu/Cut® Systems
Page designer: LeNae Gerig for Hot Off The Press

This is the easiest pocket to make—simply cut a slit in the center of the cork board paper, then glue a plain sheet of paper to the back. Like the page on 89, a page like this could be created for each year by varying the color, journaling and cutouts or Punch-Outs™ used.

Paper Pizazz™: cork board, books & pencils (*School Days*)
Solid Paper Pizazz™: blue (*Solid Jewel Tones*), green, yellow (*Plain Brights*)
Cutouts: large tack, "My Favorites," "Hooray for You" (*School Days*)
Decorative scissors: Victorian by Fiskars®, Inc.
Page designer: Carol Dace

Pockets don't have to cover the entire page. Make this one with a 6"x8" rectangle and a matted top, then place a card inside. The Father's Day paper adds color and reinforces the page theme. A similar page could be made using Mother's Day paper from Paper Pizazz™ Our Holidays & Seasons (see below) and using "MOM" on the pocket. (Pocket pattern on page 139.)

Paper Pizazz™: Father's Day (*Holidays & Seasons*)
Solid Paper Pizazz™: green, blue (*Plain Brights*)
Decorative scissors: sunflower by Fiskars®, Inc.
Page designer: Carol Dace

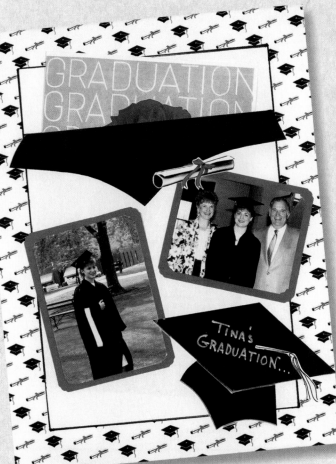

When making pocket pages, treat the pocket like any other large page element. If it's not the focus of the page, then other items need to draw interest. The pocket on this page is simply another background element; however, the pocket flap and announcement are important so the photos shouldn't overlap these parts. (Pocket pattern on page 139.)

Paper Pizazz™: graduation (*School Days*)
Solid Paper Pizazz™: black (*Solid Jewel Tones*), red (*Plain Brights*), white (*Plain Pastels*)
Cutouts: diploma roll (*School Days*)
Mortar board die cut: Accu/Cut® Systems
White pen: Zig® Opaque Writer by EK Success Ltd.
Page designer: Carol Dace

© & ™ Accu/Cut® Systems

Strips

Strips easily focus attention and add color! Like matting, strips direct the eye to a particular part of the page. Compare the "before" page to the page at the left and the difference a few strips of paper can make.

Paper Pizazz™: ivy, bachelor's buttons, white rose buds (*Floral Papers*)
Solid Paper Pizazz™: metallic gold (*Metallic Papers*), deep blue (*Solid Muted Colors*)
Decorative scissors: deckle wave, deckle by Family Treasures
Page designer: Katie Hacker for Hot Off The Press

before

before

Before the strips were added (see above) this page was pretty plain and slightly too even—no part of it was accented to draw attention. With the double-matted strips, the viewer's eye naturally drifts downward and right, ensuring that all the photos and journaling are viewed.

Paper Pizazz™: blue & green stripes, purple ripple (*Great Backgrounds*)
Solid Paper Pizazz™: green, lime, blue, yellow, aqua (*Solid Bright Papers*)
Decorative scissors: deckle by Fiskars®, Inc.
Page designer: Katie Hacker for Hot Off The Press

Strips make great headlines. This 2" wide pink dotted paper is matted twice, then a 1" blue strip is centered on top. The matted strip is the perfect place to add Pooh letters. Mat the photos with the same papers you used for the headline strip.

Paper Pizazz™: Pooh & Piglet (*Fun Days with Pooh*), tri dots on pink (*Dots, Checks, Plaids & Stripes*)

Solid Paper Pizazz™: mint, goldenrod, blue (*Plain Pastels*)

Punch-Outs™: letters (*Pooh ABC*), Pooh & Piglet (*Pooh*)

Decorative scissors: ripple by Fiskars®, Inc.

Page designer: Katie Hacker for Hot Off The Press

Disney characters © Disney Enterprises, Inc.

Like other page elements, strips need to be varied to be effective. If everything is the same size and weight, it can become boring! Strips of different widths create a slightly off-center page, which contrasts with the regular size and placement of these photos. The blue matting on the large strip connects it to the thin strip, drawing the eye across the page. Notice all the shapes used here—circle, oval, rectangle and diamond!

Paper Pizazz™: red dots & lines (*Bright Great Backgrounds*), bikes & wagons (*Child's Play*)

Solid Paper Pizazz™: blue, goldenrod (*Plain Brights*)

Punch-Outs™: wagon (*Kids*)

Decorative scissors: ripple by Fiskars®, Inc.

Page designer: LeNae Gerig for Hot Off The Press

131

Matting isn't the only way to embellish strips. Make these using decorative scissors and a bow punch. The patterned papers form the background, strips and matting. Photo Friends Punch-Outs™ are meant to wrap around photos; they adorn the photos and journaling to add extra Christmas spirit.

Paper Pizazz™: red & green dots, green plaid (*Ho Ho Ho!!!*), white dot on green (*Christmas*)

Solid Paper Pizazz™: red (*Plain Brights*), white (*Plain Pastels*)

Punch-Outs™: Santa, elf, snowman and soldier (*Photo Friends*)

Bow punch: McGill, Inc.

Decorative scissors: deckle, colonial by Fiskars®, Inc.

Red pen: Zig® Writer by EK Success Ltd.

Page designer: Debbie Peterson

© & ™ Accu/Cut® Systems

The papers used on this page are all 12"x12" papers; after the blue, green and brown papers have been used for matting, a little will be left over. Turn them into strips. Combining three narrow strips has them working as one large strip. Weave the strips at the upper left corner for a nice final touch.

Paper Pizazz™: ferns on handmade, green handmade, blue handmade, brown handmade, (*Handmade Look Papers*)

Leaf die cuts: Accu/Cut® Systems

Decorative scissors: deckle by Fiskars®, Inc.

Page designer: Katie Hacker for Hot Off The Press

Because the tie dye paper is slightly different in each area, each strip is matted in a separate color, creating a feeling of spinning toward the photos.

Paper Pizazz™: bright bubbles, tie dye (*Bright Great Backgrounds*)

Solid Paper Pizazz™: purple, green, orange, light green, light orange (*Plain Brights*)

Punch-Outs™: "Special Times" (*Title*)

Decorative scissors: deckle by Family Treasures

Page designer: Katie Hacker for Hot Off The Press

As on the page above, these plain strips focus attention inward. The photos, each matted differently, expand outward from the center postcard with elf Punch-Outs™ joining the images to create flow from photo to photo. Notice the photos opposite each other are matted similarly, but each photo has its own style.

Paper Pizazz™: green with white stars (*Stripes, Checks & Dots*), red & white stripes (*Ho Ho Ho!!!*)

Solid Paper Pizazz™: red (*Solid Brights*), hunter green, dark blue (*Solid Jewel Tones*)

Punch-Outs™: elves, postcard (*Christmas*)

Decorative scissors: jigsaw by Fiskars®, Inc.

Page designer: LeNae Gerig for Hot Off The Press

Embellish the lattice background paper with thin strips designed to imitate trellis plants. The narrow wavy strips work to form a trellised stem, while the punches create flowers. The large green paper works almost like a strip, dividing the page into smaller areas and the rectangular shapes of the photos and journaling divide the green further.

Paper Pizazz™: green handmade, purple handmade (*Handmade Papers*) lattice (*Our Wedding Day*)

Solid Paper Pizazz™: pink (*Plain Brights*), hunter green (*Solid Muted Tones*)

⁵⁄₁₆", ⅜" and 1" wide flower punches: Family Treasures

½" and 1" long leaf punches: McGill, Inc.

Circle punch: Marvy® Uchida

Decorative scissors: wave, deckle by Family Treasures

Page designer: Becky Goughnour for Hot Off The Press

Don't use strips merely as accents! The Great American Pastime and the American flag are handily joined by using baseballs paper for the background, then adding corrugated red strips to it. After adding the blue field, decorate it with a baseball surrounded by stars. It's a home run!

Paper Pizazz™: base balls (*Sports*)

Solid Paper Pizazz™: blue (*Solid Jewel Tones*), red (*Plain Brights*), white (*Plain Pastels*)

Baseball die cut: Ellison® Craft & Design

½" wide star punch: All Night Media®, Inc.

Corrugator: Fiskars®, Inc.

Computer typeface: D.J. Inkers™

Red pen: Zig® Writer by EK Success Ltd.

Page designer: Kristy Banks for Pebbles in my Pocket

Sometimes using papers is a lot like using watercolors—you add color on top of color until you achieve the effect you are looking for. Here, the watercolor reflections strips introduces new shades to the pink background, which allows the next layers to add additional colors which separate the photos from the background.

Paper Pizazz™: watercolor reflections (*Great Backgrounds*), fuzzy spirals (*Bright Great Backgrounds*)
Solid Paper Pizazz™: blue, purple (*Plain Pastels*)
Spiral punch: McGill, Inc.
Decorative scissors: leaf by Fiskars®, Inc.
Page designer: LeNae Gerig for Hot Off The Press

Because the photos are black and white, it's important to use colored papers to introduce the school colors. Weave ¾" wide black strips and ¼" wide yellow strips as shown. Mat the letter, class year and photos, then arrange on the background. Tip: to make a letter from your school, trace the letter from your jacket to use as a pattern.

Solid Paper Pizazz™: light orange (*Plain Brights*), white (*Plain Pastels*), black, gray (*Solid Jewel Tones*)
Decorative scissors: deckle by Family Treasures
Page designer: Heather Hummel

By using strips of the friendly bugs paper, instead of the entire page as a background, you can make many pages from the one sheet. In addition, the frog and snail strips help answer the question "What are little boys made of?"

Paper Pizazz™: friendly bugs (*Child's Play*)
Solid Paper Pizazz™: hunter green, red (*Solid Jewel Tones*), brown, tan, blue (*Solid Muted Colors*)
Alphabet stickers: Frances Meyer, Inc.®
Page designer: Ann Smith for Memory Lane

Combine strips to make a frame. As above, the It's a Boy! paper has rows of designs which is great for cutting into strips. Each strip on this page has three lines of text with the ends cut at an angle to make a frame. Mat the frame on blue paper, then on white. Place the photo in the center and glue it to a blue background page. Use stickers to spell the baby's name in 1" wide blocks along the lower page. The dots and rattles on the sides are hand-drawn embellishments—aren't they cute?

Paper Pizazz™: It's a Boy! (*Baby*)
Solid Paper Pizazz™: light blue, white (*Plain Pastels*)
Alphabet stickers: Pebbles Inc.
Blue and white pens: Zig® Writer by EK Success Ltd.
Page designer: Terri Carter for Paper Hearts

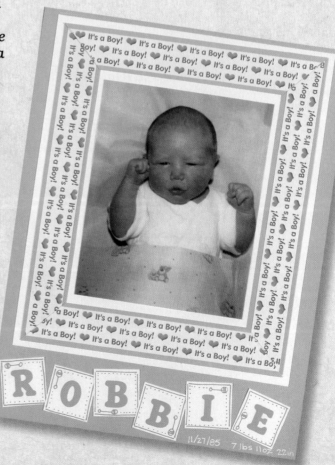

When a paper has a strong repeating pattern, it can be cut apart to make a larger page. Cut this 8½"x11" page into strips, then decide where your photos will go. Insert the strips under the photos as shown, hiding the ends under the photos. No one will be able to tell you didn't use 12" strips!

Paper Pizazz™: trick or treat stripes (*Special Days with Pooh*), white dot on black (*Dots, Checks, Plaids & Stripes*)
Solid Paper Pizazz™: light orange (*Plain Brights*), black (*Solid Jewel Tones*), orange (*Solid Bright Papers*)
Bat punch: Family Treasures
Bat die cut: Accu/Cut® Systems
White pen: Zig® Opaque Writer by EK Success Ltd.
Decorative scissors: bat wings by Fiskars®, Inc.
Page designer: LeNae Gerig for Hot Off The Press

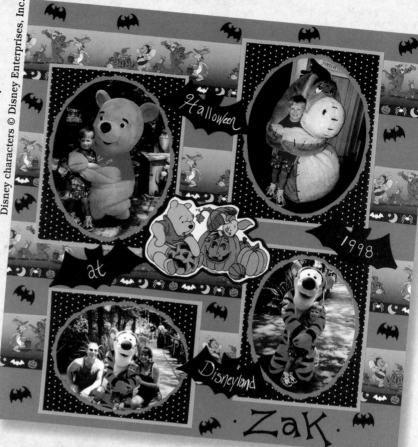

Like the page above, this paper has been cut apart and separated to make a larger page. Mat the strips to take up more space and use the center piece as a mat for a special photo.

Paper Pizazz™: colorful dots on black (*Stripes, Checks & Dots*), picnic stamps (*Disney's Mickey and The Old Gang*)
Solid Paper Pizazz™: yellow (*Plain Brights*), black (*Solid Jewel Tones*)
White pen: Zig® Opaque Writer by EK Success Ltd.
Decorative scissors: ripple by Fiskars®, Inc.
Page designer: LeNae Gerig for Hot Off The Press

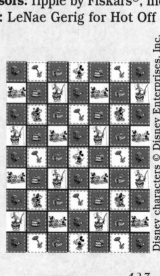

moon, page 56

tree, page 89

lava lamp, page 102

nutcracker, page 96

pocket top, page 129

marker, page 98

sign, page 98

pocket top,
page 129

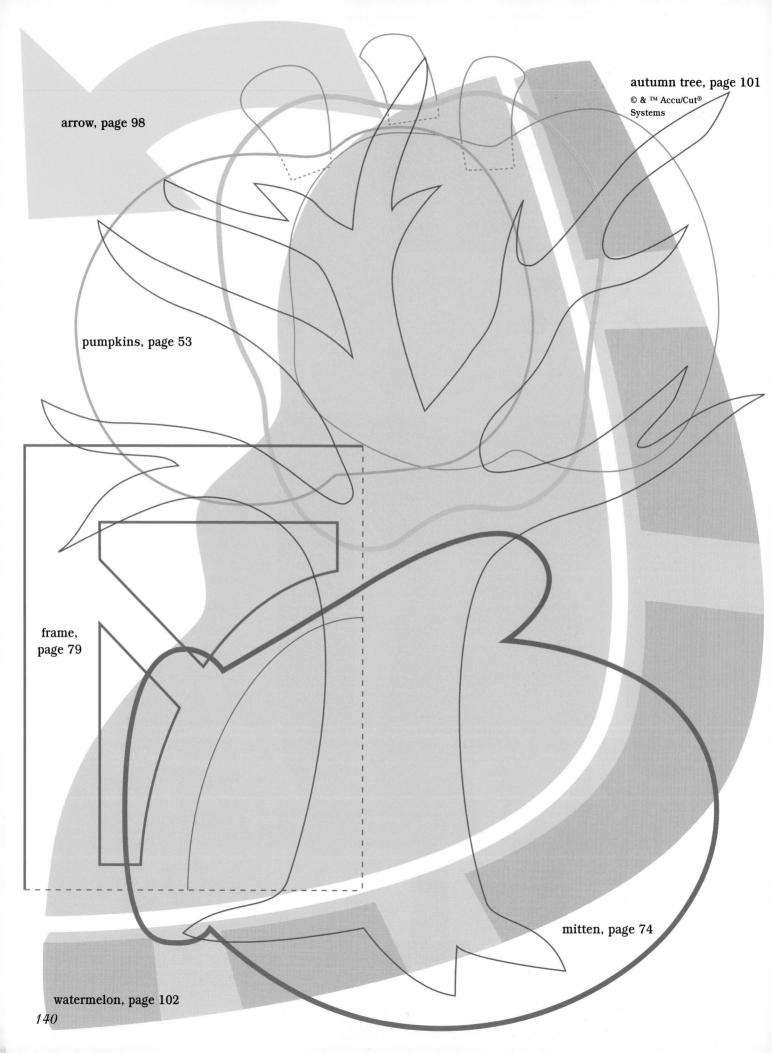

arrow, page 98

autumn tree, page 101

pumpkins, page 53

frame,
page 79

mitten, page 74

watermelon, page 102

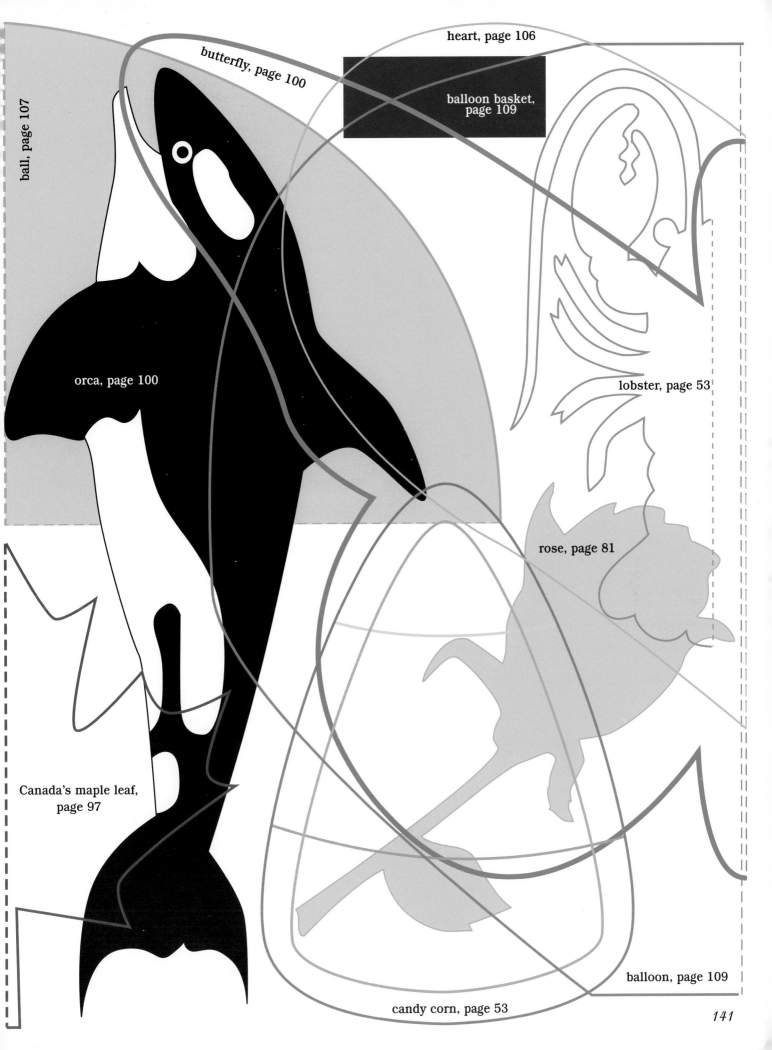

ball, page 107

butterfly, page 100

heart, page 106

balloon basket,
page 109

orca, page 100

lobster, page 53

rose, page 81

Canada's maple leaf,
page 97

balloon, page 109

candy corn, page 53

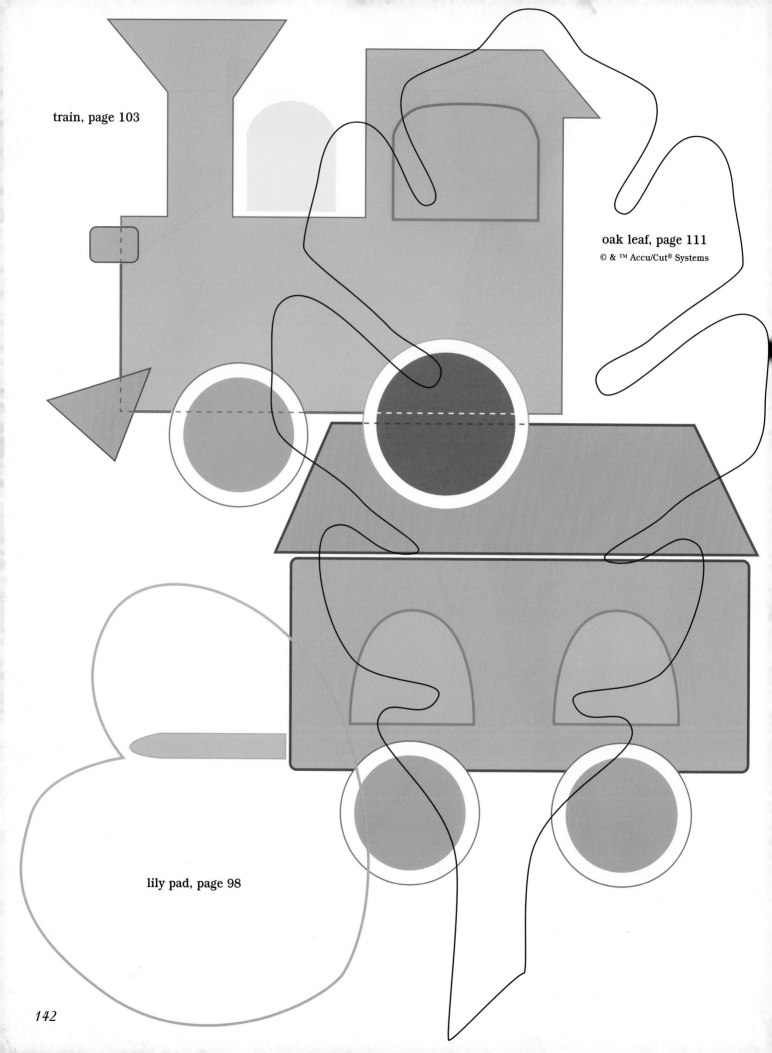

train, page 103

oak leaf, page 111
© & ™ Accu/Cut® Systems

lily pad, page 98

142

Glossary

Acid-free
Acid is used in paper manufacturing to break apart the wood fibers and the lignin which holds them together. If acid remains in the materials used for photo albums, the acid can react chemically with photographs and accelerate their deterioration. Acid-free products have a pH factor of 7 to 8.5. It's imperative that all materials (glue, pens, paper, etc.) used in memory albums or scrapbooks be acid-free.

Acid migration
is the transfer of acidity from one item to another through physical contact or acidic vapors. If a newspaper clipping were put into an album, the area it touched would turn yellow or brown. A de-acidification spray can be used on acidic papers, or they can be color photocopied onto acid-free papers.

Archival quality
is a term used to indicate materials which have undergone laboratory analysis to determine that their acidic and buffered content is within safe levels.

Buffered Paper
During manufacture a buffering agent such as calcium carbonate or magnesium bicarbonate can be added to paper to neutralize acid contaminants. Such papers have a pH of 8.5.

Cropping
Cutting or trimming a photo to keep only the most important parts. See pages 10–11 for cropping ideas and information about cropping Polaroid photos.

Journaling
refers to the text on a scrapbook page giving details about the photographs. Journaling can be done in your own handwriting or with adhesive letters, rub-ons, etc. It is probably the most important part of memory albums.

Lignin
is the bonding material which holds wood fibers together as a tree grows. If lignin remains in the final paper product (as with newsprint) it will become yellow and brittle over time. Most paper other than newsprint is lignin-free.

pH factor
refers to the acidity of a paper. The pH scale is the standard for measurement of acidity and alkalinity. It runs from 0 to 14 with each number representing a ten-fold increase; pH neutral is 7. Acid-free products have a pH factor from 7 to 8.5. Special pH tester pens are available to help you determine the acidity or alkalinity of products.

Photo-safe
is a term similar to archival quality but more specific to materials used with photographs. Acid-free is the determining factor for a product to be labeled photo-safe.

Sheet protectors
These are made of plastic to slip over a finished album page. They can be side-loading or top-loading and fit 8½"x11" or 12"x12" pages. It is important that they be acid-free. Polypropylene is commonly used—never use vinyl sheet protectors.

Manufacturers & Suppliers:

Accu/Cut® Systems
1035 E. Dodge St.
Fremont, NE 68025

All Night Media®, Inc.
Post Office Box 10607
San Rafael, CA 94912

C-Thru® Ruler Co.
6 Britton Dr.
Bloomfield, CT 06002

Canson-Talens, Inc.
21 Industrial Dr.
S. Hadley, MA 01075

Chatterbox, Inc.
P.O. Box 216
Star, ID 83669

Close to My Heart
1199 West 700 South
Pleasant Grove, UT 84062

C.M. Offray & Son, Inc.
Route 24, Box 601
Chester, NJ 07930

D. J. Inkers™
Post Office Box 2462
Sandy, UT 84091

Deja Views™ by C-Thru®
6 Britton Dr.
Bloomfield, CT 06002

EK Success Ltd.
611 Industrial Rd.
Carlstadt, NJ 07072

Ellison® Craft & Design
Toll Free 888-972-7238
714-724-0555

Extra Special Products Corp.
Post Office Box 777
Greenville, OH 45331

Family Treasures, Inc.
24922 Anza Dr., Unit D
Valencia, CA 91355

Fiskars®, Inc.
7811 W. Stewart Avenue
Wausau, WI 54401

Frances Meyer Inc.®
Post Office Box 3088
Savannah, GA 31402

The Gifted Line®
800-5-GIFTED
FAX 510-215-4772

Hambly Studios, Inc.
941 George St.
Santa Clara, CA 95054

Hot Off The Press, Inc.
1250 NW Third, Dept B
Canby, OR 97013
503-266-9102

Keeping Memories Alive™
260 N. Main
Spanish Fork, UT 84660

Making Memories™
Post Office Box 1188
Centerville, UT 84014

Marvy® Uchida
3535 Del Amo Blvd
Torrance, CA 90503

McGill, Inc.
Post Office Box 177
Marengo, IL 60152

Mrs. Grossman's Paper Company
Post Office Box 4467
Petaluma, CA 94955

Pebbles Inc.
P.O. Box 489
Orem, UT 84058

Provo Craft®
285 E. 900 South
Provo, UT 84606

Rubber Stampede
P.O. Box 246
Berkeley, CA 94701

SpotPen™
Post Office Box 1559
Las Cruces, NM 88004

Stampendous!®
1357 S. Lewis St.
Anaheim, CA 92805

StenSource International, Inc.
18971 Hess Avenue
Sonora, CA 95370

Stickopotamus™ by EK Success Ltd.
611 Industrial Rd.
Carlstadt, NJ 07072

Westrim® Crafts
9667 Canoga Avenue
Chatsworth, CA 91311

Retail Stores:

Memory Lane
700 E. Southern Avenue
Mesa, AZ 85204

Pebbles in my Pocket
Orem, UT 801-226-2632
St. George, UT 435-656-5857

Paper Hearts
6185 Highland Drive
Salt Lake City, UT 84121

Scrapbook Magazines:

Creating Keepsakes
888-247-5282

Memory Makers
800-366-6465